# No, My Darling Daughter

Melissa's mother was due to arrive in half an hour for one of their many long-postponed lunch dates. With Calvin gone, Dominic lingered, unwilling to be dispatched posthaste.

"My dear girl," he said, "Surely your mother knows you have love affairs. I can't see why you're all nerves."

"Since I am a veteran of marriage," Melissa said with annoyance, "she knows I am not exactly a virgin, but I can't very well flaunt you before her."

Dominic grinned. "Your mother should be pleased that you have a considerate lover like me who doesn't desert you after getting what he wants, as you Americans so quaintly say, leaving you lonely and sobbing in the dark, but instead holds you and cossets you like a cherished being until morning."

"Dominic, please get out of here. Now! She's coming at 11:30 . . ."

"Maybe your mother will like me. How do you know? Why don't we wait and see?"

"Dominic . . . please . . . please . . . *please leave!* PLEASE, Do

D1563980

We will send you a free catalog on request. Any titles not in your local book store can be purchased by mail. Send the price of the book plus 50¢ shipping charge to Leisure Books, P.O. Box 270, Norwalk, Connecticut 06852.

Titles currently in print are available for industrial and sales promotion at reduced rates. Address inquiries to Nordon Publications, Inc., Two Park Avenue, New York, New York 10016, Attention: Premium Sales Department.

# MOTHERS
## and
# LOVERS

**Jeannie Sakol**

LEISURE BOOKS • NEW YORK CITY

Other books by Jeannie Sakol:

THE INEPT SEDUCER
GUMDROP, GUMDROP, LET DOWN YOUR HAIR
I WAS NEVER THE PRINCESS
NEW YEAR'S EVE
FLORA SWEET
ALL DAY, ALL NIGHT, ALL WOMAN
PROMISE ME ROMANCE
THE WONDERFUL WORLD OF COUNTRY MUSIC
HOT THIRTY

A LEISURE BOOK

Published by

Nordon Publications, Inc.
Two Park Avenue
New York, N.Y. 10016

Copyright © 1980 by Jeannie Sakol

For Roger Price
Who gave me confidence, courage, love and the gen-
erosity of his mind and humor. And taught me how
to cook and play the piano. And not to make dumb
jokes.

# PROLOGUE

## 1979

"I *hate* her!"

"She's your mother. You can't hate her."

"I don't care. I hate her anyway. She ruined my life!" Stephanie stood before Ingrid's Regency fireplace, digging the toe of a Gucci boot into Ingrid's Bokhara rug while glaring at her flushed and tousled image in Ingrid's mammoth ormolu mirror.

"Stop making a face. It'll freeze that way!"

"Oh, for God's sake, Aung Ingrid. Quit treating me like a child. It's bad enough *she* treats me like a child."

"You're acting like a child."

Stephanie stamped her foot. "I am *not*. I'm twenty four years old and I'm a married woman—until I get rid of that rat bastard, anyway—"

"Oh, Stephanie, Tom's a lovely guy—Melissa

thinks so, too—''

''My mother would love anybody who married me. She'd be nuts about the Incredible Hulk if he was her son-in-law. 'Hi, everyone, meet my over-size son-in-law!' . . .''

''Stephanie, I'm getting pissed off. Melissa's my dearest friend. And you're my dearest friend's daughter. And I won't have *you* putting the knock on her. Dig?''

''Oh, Aunt Ingrid—'' The younger woman forgot her anger long enough to hug the lean titian-haired woman she had been coming to for comfort and advice from the time she was old enough to toddle. ''I'm so unhappy.''

''I know. But have you figured out why you're so unhappy?''

''It's—everything. I don't have a job. I don't have a marriage. Tom is driving me crazy—''

''Why don't you talk things over with Melissa? She's your mother. She wants you to be happy.''

''Don't make me laugh.''

''Believe me, kid. She's your mother. I was there when you were born.''

''You know what I mean. Just because she ruined her own life is no reason to ruin mine, is it?''

''Stephanie!'' Ingrid's mellifluous voice had a hard edge. ''Sit down!''

''Look, Aung Ingrid—''

''Sit down before I knock you down!''

Stephanie sat down. ''Don't get hostile.''

''You're the one who's hostile and I've had it up to here! Your mother is a warm and wonderful woman. She's made plenty of mistakes. She's fought lots of battles and she's won a lot of them. She's done every-thing in her power for you—except maybe take out a million dollar life insurance policy and then jump off the George Washington Bridge.''

"Come *on*! That's not what I'm saying.''

"Well, the hell *are* you saying?''

"I'm saying—'' Stephanie suddenly collapsed into a sobbing mound of blonde hair, cashmere and leather. Her words were a garbled gusher of sobs and accu-sations. "I'm saying she made a mess of her life and a mess of her marriage and now the sins of the mother are visited on the daughter and I'm making a mess of *my* life and *my* marriage and it's all her fault!''

Ingrid poured them each a Harvey's Bristol Cream.

"No thanks,'' Stephanie moaned.

"Drink it! You'll fall into a drunken coma and forget everything.''

Stephanie took a grudging sip.

"Okay, Princess, let's start from the top. What's your beef?''

"You know everything. I don't have to tell you.''

"Of course I know everything. What I'm trying to find out is how much *you* know.''

"I know my father loved her a lot and she dumped him and I know I loved her a lot and she dumped *me*.''

"That's just not so, Stephanie.''

"She never loved my father. She used him as a stud. He told me so. All she wanted was to get pregnant and then she had no more use for him.''

"How can you say these things? That's simply not so, believe me, Stephanie.''

"And I'm just like her. I'm using Tom as a stud. And now—I can't look at him. I can't stand to have him near me. I—Oh, Aunt Ingrid—''

''What, darling? Please, for God's sake, tell me! It's not—cancer or anything like that?''

''I'm pregnant! And I don't know whether to—''

''Oh, darling—Melissa will be so—''

''Don't talk to me about Melissa. I know what Melissa did. Dad's never forgiven her.''

''That isn't quite accurate.''

''Don't tell me. I know.''

Ingrid stared down at her best friend's daughter and took a deep breath. ''You *don't* know. And maybe it's time you did know what it was like in New York in the early fifties. God, a quarter of a century ago! Twenty five years. Hard to believe. Your mother and I were even younger than you. We thought we were pretty hot stuff and we wanted so much. Love. Happiness. A beautiful future.''

Ingrid's eyes moved to a silver framed photograph of two young women in short cap hairdoes and enormous hoop earrings, Melissa giggling self-consciously, Ingrid already the professional model, cool and perfectly posed.

''She and Max split the day this was taken.''

''Is that why she was laughing?''

Ingrid sat down beside Stephanie and took her hands in a tight clasp. ''Your mother had to fight for survival and sanity and pride. Now, you are going to sit still without a peep or a crack while I tell you exactly what it was like and exactly what happened.''

# FRIDAY

The doorbell.

"Don't answer," he said.

"No."

"Even if it's a telegram."

"No."

"Or the Fuller Brush man with free samples."

"No."

"We don't care."

"No."

"About anything."

"No."

"Jesus—you're a good looking piece of meat all right. Stretched out like that. And all you can say is No! Jesus—No! No! No!"

He traced the spiral paths of both ears.

"Now do you say No?"

"No."

Descending the neck wall, finger-over-finger to the sloping plateau of chest.

"Now do you say NO? Still No? No?"

"No."

Pulses down, his wrists made a throbbing connection with the touchpoints newly alert for the contact, like that child's educational game where the right wire pressed to the right button gives off a buzzing sound and a slight, pleasant shock.

"Now, will you still say No?"

"No."

"No? No? The double negative makes a positive. I'll bet you didn't know *that*, did you?"

"No."

Proceeding with the middle fingertip of each hand poised on the electrical charge points, he moved in parallel lines down her rib cage, fingers fanned, pausing either side of the umbilical cave where another button, a once-was button, was now inverted, pulled inside, out of sight.

"Now will you say No? Now? No?"

"No."

He crossed the demarcation line where winter white turns to summer tan, fumbling for the last button . . . the lost button . . . the key button to the entire mechanism . . . the control center of the whole intricate switchboard.

Button, button, who's got the button? Who wants the button?

"And NOW? No . . . Baby, no?"

"No—no—no, no, no . . ."

"Now? And now! And NOW! AND NOW!"

"No . . . no, no, no, no, no—NO, NO, NO, NO-OO! . . ."

*N-N-N-nnnnnnnnnnnnn.* All motion had stopped. What was that sound? Was it the echo of her own

12

voice, screaming to wrench free from that last orgasmic throb?

Or was the doorbell screaming again? Or had the doorbell been screaming unheard all along, another urgent finger on another button, shrieking its demand to be answered?

"Somebody's still out there," he said, reaching for a cigarette.

"Shut up! It'll go away." Unable to move, she suddenly remembered a magazine ad for a device you can clamp on a book that projects each page onto the ceiling.

"Who do you think it is?"

"Who cares? It could be the laundryman—"

"Or the groceryman—"

"Or the telephone man—"

"Jesus—that reminds me. I better call the office. What time is it?" he asked.

"Three o'clock." She could see her watch behind his head.

"I better move! Got a meeting at four. New client!"

"I better get a move on myself," she said. "Tea at the Plaza!" she announced grandly. "I've been roped into serving on some half-assed committee."

Save The Wombat Federation, or something like that. She could thank Ingrid for strong-arming her into it. Committees were good for their social standing, Ingrid said. Committees got your picture in the paper.

"It'll take me a few minutes to dress, Sweetie. Why don't you be a good boy and fix yourself a drink, and I'll give you the large honor of dropping me off," she said. "You're a darling and you'll save me a fortune in cab fare."

13

"Can't, Angel. But let me buy you a cab." He flipped a bill on the table and finished dressing.

*Didn't he want a shower?* The hell with him. Let him offend the new client. *Tant pis!*

"Sorry we didn't have time for lunch, Melissa. Next time, huh Baby? Oh—and about that problem of yours. Let me see what I can do, huh?"

He stumbled down the narrow flight of stairs, opened the front door and tripped over the package propped against it.

"There's your doorbell." He kicked it inside and slammed the door.

"Son of a bitch!"

Still naked, she snaked down the stairs and picked up the package. Was it a present? God!—more books! Those book clubs never gave up. Once you signed the culture coupon, you were cross-indexed and coded for life. Peering around the living room door, she hurled the parcel to the couch some twelve feet away. In her bare state, she dared not enter the room because the drapes were open and anyone strolling along East 50th Street this beautiful spring afternoon would be able to look in and see her playing September Morn terribly out of season.

Back upstairs, she started her tub, wrapped her blonde-streaked hair in a red plaid turban and darted back to the bedroom just long enough to take the phone off the hook so she could bathe in peace. Otherwise, if the phone rang she would have to leap out and splash footprints over everything. Or let the answering service pick up. But that meant calling the answering service when she got out of the tub and that meant an extra call on her phone bill which was high enough now.

14

Also, some people didn't like to leave messages and might not wait for the service to answer.

With the phone off, anyone calling would get a busy signal and try again. You couldn't leave the phone off too long, though, because somebody inevitably reported it to the operator who would listen in and know what you were doing. The phone company frowned on this kind of social insurance.

Melissa couldn't bear to miss a phone call, even Lord & Taylor to say they had the dress she wanted or McCall's to renew her subscription. Talking on the telephone stimulated her. Its shiny blackness held the promise of joy and opportunity as yet unknown. At any moment, it might disconnect the old life, the old number, the wrong number and give her instead a bright, new exchange, one that had never belonged to anyone else and did not echo with ghosts of whimperings and sobbings and pleadings and metallic laughter and spiteful clicks that cracked the inner ear.

"When you're not with me, the phone is your mouth," Max had once said to her before they were married, calling her in the early morning from this very bedroom. "It connects me to you and when I kiss your voice coming through it, I'm connected to you."

That was before. This was after. The bedroom and the phone were hers now, without Max.

She sank chin-deep into Crepe de Chine bubbles floating like whipped cream around her. It was like being in a huge porcelain coffee cup. How many spoonfuls of instant Maxwell House would it take to make all this nice hot water into coffee?

15

She would just lie there with a book, sipping through a glass straw.

*"Do you suffer from coffee bath nerves?"*

Or, *"What are you doing?"*

*"Oh, I'm just having my morning coffee. I'm limiting myself to one cup a day."*

The compulsive home decorator might have tubs designed as period cups, everything from the cherubic limoges of the French kings to the chipped functionalism of the Automat.

Testimonial: *It's the BATH-I-E-R Coffee*!

The idea began to pall. Methodically, she began to wash, using a hand brush to scrub all grime-collecting surfaces, ankle bones, heels, elbows and knuckles.

The slob! Not even lunch! She threw the brush against the wall in her anger but instead of plopping back into the tub, it ricocheted onto the floor. She couldn't quite reach it and had to get out.

"I'm so hungry, I could eat soap."

She had called him this morning because his father was a city commissioner who might be able to pull some strings and save her from being evicted from this house. One of the few remaining carriage houses in mid-Manhattan, it had been sold recently to a real estate combine. They wanted her out so they could get in and make their investment pay.

There had been a hearing but a young divorcee with no children living on alimony and trying to hang onto a low-rent bargain was not exactly a picture to melt the heart of a civil servant.

The eviction notice had not yet come but it hung over the door like an upside down horse-shoe. As one of her wilder schemes for staying here, she had hoped his father might be able to pigeon-hole the eviction indefinitely or contrive some other delaying action.

"Let's have a little drink here before we go to lunch," he had said, the warning flag up. "I brought some good gin."

Then there was the business of getting out the ice, stirring up the martinis without bruising the booze and sitting down on the couch.

"You know I want to help you," he'd kept assuring her, sincerely.

*So why not do something for me?*

"You know I'd do anything for you."

*So how about doing something for me?*

"You know etc. etc. etc. etc."

*So why not etc. etc. etc. etc.?*

So why not?

So she had done something for him in the coldest, most clinically dispassionate way she had ever experienced. A new kind of kicks. Negative pleasure. No. No. Nooooo. Dissonant music in the lowest possible key.

And even while she was doing it for him, she knew he couldn't and wouldn't do anything for her. Bad judgment on her part, pure and simple, like entertaining people for dinner who will never invite you back in a million years.

She could forgive him for not trying to help her. Why the hell should he, really? He had problems of his own, the not-too-sharp son of a political boss, the weak dropping of a savage racehorse.

But to do her out of lunch, too, was unforgivable. That he was a good athlete did in no way satisfy woman's primary need—food. He made love with the

17

grandstand bravura of a tennis pro, the kind who is all technique with brilliant service and masterly control but who can never arouse the emotions.

Dripping wet, she pulled on a terry cloth burnoose, replaced the phone and ran down the stairs to the kitchen, the heavy towel fabric rubbing her dry by friction as she moved.

Three thirty! Dammit—she'd have to take a cab after all. Swearing off taxis was harder than cigarettes. No matter what time you started, you only had five minutes to get there.

Racing back upstairs with a glass of milk and a slab of brown bread thick with peanut butter, she began to dress. Pale grey suit. Frothy white jabot. Small, black hat and *the* one and only mink stole. Fluff at the neck and a touch of fur photographed best, according to Ingrid, and Ingrid knew more about photographs than most photographers.

She had just finished inking in one eyelid when the doorbell rang. My God! Had he come back? This time with his father?

She leaned out the bedroom window. It was Ingrid, incredibly blonde, angular and beautiful. An emaciated Viking. So Scandinavian were her face and coloring, it was hard to believe she had begun life in the Bronx as Anna Maria Curzio.

"Hi!" Melissa called, tossing down her doorkey. "I only have one eye. Come on up and tell me the latest malicious gossip."

Ingrid perched on a stool in the doorway of Melissa's tiny dressing room.

"You're a darling to come by for me," Melissa said, grimacing into the mirror. "I can't seem to get

18

ready on time anymore. Lately I've been getting up—and then it's lunchtime—and then I lump around or something and it's drink time. And then suddenly it's three o'clock in the morning and another day gone to hell!''

"Did you have lunch in today?"

"Don't remind me!" Melissa said balefully. "I had a date with some guy whose father is bigsville with the city administration and I thought maybe he could do something about my eviction. His idea of lunch was to bring a bottle of gin and his track shoes, cha-cha-cha!''

"How terribly square and unimaginative! The No-Cal Cavalier!" Ingrid commiserated. "Obviously has no instinct for the finer things . . .''

Melissa felt victimized by the unknown. A Kafka lady. Somebody out there loathed her, wanted to take away her comfortable low-rent home. As it was she could barely skin through on the seventy-five-dollar a week alimony Max gave her. It was just enough money not to have to work, but not enough money to enjoy not working.

"Come on, Honey. Don't be depressed!" Ingrid said briskly. "What's happening? Getting any work?"

"Yes—and no," Melissa said wryly. "Too bad I haven't got your skinny bones. Maybe I could be a model, too.''

She sighed, but without rancor. Melissa had no special talents, no burning ambitions, no real skills. Charming, resourceful, quick, she was the ideal Girl Friday with a dabbler's interest in fashions, ceramics and interior decor. After several months of trying, she found that free-lance assignments in these areas were

19

few and far between. People loved having you shove their furniture around on a rainy Sunday, but not if they had to pay you for it!

She couldn't brood about that now. "Ingrid, this suit needs something—a pin, maybe."

While her friend ran an experienced hand through the jungle of costume jewelry, Melissa changed the subject.

"What's with Bernard? Any closer to the Big Question?"

"*Quelle chance*!" Ingrid snapped vehemently, pinning a deep topaz oval to Melissa's lapel. "Today, for instance. Friday—right? We've gone out on Friday night every week for the past three months—right? So this week, what happens? I could *spit*! He waits until late last night—very late, I might add—to tell me that *tonight* he's having dinner at his mother's house—the Park Avenue ghetto. The old girl suddenly rediscovered the Jewish Sabbath! Big deal! What does he expect me to do—stand up and cheer?"

Melissa knew that Ingrid was more hurt than angry. As the Cover Girl darling of Newport, Westport and every other damned port from the Hamptons to Palm Beach, her mild flirtations with society fags masquerading as bachelors were one thing. Finding a rich, respectable husband was something else. Bernard Nahoum was very definitely that something else.

"Don't let Bernard *or* his mother get you down!" Melissa said soothingly as Ingrid wrapped a rope of pearls around her wrist.

Mothers! She remembered how Max's mother had come sneaking over to this very house one morning before they were married (very early, of course) and

20

found Melissa wearing his bathrobe and cooking his breakfast.

The memory still burnt. What had she expected? They were engaged. What did his mother think they did every night, play Scrabble? They way that old lady carried on, you'd have thought they were stealing. And Max hadn't even defended himself. Oh, no.

"Yes, Mother," was all he'd said, promising like a little boy caught at the cookie jar not to do that dirty thing again until they were married—and the wedding six months away!

"Pearls no good." Ingrid unwound them quickly. "Pin is enough. Let's get out of here. Late."

Melissa bit her lip, unable to shake the memory of Max and his mother and the terrible thing that had happened soon afterwards, the terrible thing for which she would never forgive Max's mother, or Max himself.

"By the way, Missy," Ingrid said casually, as they gathered up their things. "Guess who I *am* seeing tonight?"

"Who?"

"Philip Winston!" She avoided her friend's startled gaze.

"I thought you'd stopped seeing him," Melissa said archly, swinging her mink stole over one shoulder. "Particularly when he finessed your marriage-or-else ploy."

Dig, dig, dig.

"Tonight is for old times' sake," Ingrid smiled. "And if anything uncouth happens—well, I can blame it on dear old Bernard for deserting me!"

21

Ingrid turned and clattered down the stairs, Melissa close behind, as the doorbell rang.

"Oop, I forgot my gloves!" Melissa cried, turning back. "Open it, will you?"

"Mrs. Kempton?"

Walter Simpson was a runner-up Man of Distinction. Given any choice at all, he'd have preferred being the madcap rake of the Thirties when heroes wore tails, cracked wise and drove girls home at dawn in stolen milk wagons.

Now, at 55, he had a sun-lamp tan, golfclub thumbs and a grey crewcut clipped with privet hedge skill by an English barber who charged two dollars a throw. Clenched in his absurdly white teeth was a Charatan pipe, an 0120 Lumberman but custom-made a fraction longer in the shank, a fraction wider in the bowl than the catalogue model. He smoked with the impudent nonchalance of a yacht ad, pipe bowl tilted down so that the initiated might see the C.P.—for Charatan Pipe—etched in white on the under-stem.

"No, I'm not Mrs. Kempton."

Ingrid smiled with professional admiration of a strong jawline and good shoulders.

"I'm Miss Gaard. Ingrid Gaard?"

Her inflection said, *Surely you've heard of me*?

"Haven't I seen you somewhere before? The cover of *Vogue* maybe?" he said with the assurance of a man who reads *Playboy* and knows how to handle women.

"Which you read avidly, I'm sure," Ingrid simpered, a shade sarcastic. "That may be a very successful line you have, but this time it happens to be

22

true. I do happen to be on the cover of *Vogue* . . . the current issue . . . in a yellow hat.''

He grinned amiably. ''You got me, Miss Gaard. It usually works. Ah—then *this* must be Mrs. Kempton!''

Melissa was working the soft white kid over her fingers one at a time. ''Why, yes. I'm Mrs. Kempton. . . ?''

''Well—I'm Walter Simpson.''

So? she seemed to say.

''The architect? From Kelly and Karr?'' She exchanged a puzzled stare with Ingrid. ''Are you a door-to-door architect by any chance?''

He laughed, but uncomfortably. ''You mean my office forgot to tell you I was coming this afternoon to look the property over?''

''You're from the new owners! The b—*builders* who bought this house and want to toss me out!'' Rather distantly, the lady of the manor dismissing the third gardener from her presence. ''No one bothered to call and warn me and as you can see, I'm just on my way out.''

''Yes, yes, of course,'' he apologized. ''I'm so sorry to come barging in like this.''

''It is a bit premature, I think, sending the undertaker before the body's cold. I haven't been evicted yet,'' she said.

''Mrs. Kempton,'' he protested with evident embarrassment, ''please accept my apologies. I really thought my office had fixed things up for me to look things over—''

''Does that include *me*?'' she asked tartly. He *was*

23

attractive, sort of a smudged carbon copy of Cary Grant's brother. In the right light. If you squinted.

"Not that a house and a woman haven't a lot in common," he rallied, confident in the charm of this homily he used often and with great success. Now he gave them both his two-martini smile, "It's a sweetheart of a house all right—tiny, delicate, utterly feminine. It's a shame, really, one of the oldest and smallest brownstones left in New York . . ."

*Very* attractive. Square, yes, but there was something to be said for older men and this one looked as if he took showers.

"Come on, Missy," Ingrid urged. "It's four o'clock. I'll rev up the car."

Melissa locked the front door behind them. "Well—look here, Mr. Simpson. Why don't you come back for a drink about 6:30? I'll show you the house then."

"Right!" he smiled, helping her into the bright red sportscar.

"Sorry we can't give you a lift," Ingrid shouted, accelerating with a lurch. "Only room for two!"

"He's cute!" Melissa said.

"Yeah—wonder what *his* problem is!"

Melissa said appreciatively, "Nice of Bernard to lend you his car."

"Yes. I convinced him it's easier for him to take the subway to work. Besides, red is too flashy for the banking business. Hold on! We're going to scare hell out of that cab driver!"


The committee meeting had commenced. Led by Mrs. Mariol Fredley-Pugh, chairman, plans were

24

being planned for a "Benefit Fashion Opening" of the Steuer Galleries. Proceeds would go to the Jobs for Grandma Federation, a group urging industry to hire women over 50. For publicity purposes, the project was called, ingeniously, JOG for *Just One Grandmother*.

The photographer was all set up, waiting. Mrs. Fredley-Pugh arranged herself on a couch with Mrs. Fletcher Rhinehart, childhood friend, at her right and Miss Bettijane Rhinehart, her daughter, at her left. Fanned out behind stood the remaining six members, including the two late arrivals.

From experience, Melissa knew the picture in the paper would be fuzzy, her companions indistinguishable and the caption inaccurate.

So far as she could see, pictures and squibs were about the only tangible results of all these tiresome shenanigans. Ingrid disagreed. Ingrid earnestly believed the only way to be accepted in high society was through women. The men might meet you for drinks; the women invited you to house parties. The women served on committees. Ingrid served on committees. Complete infiltration was only a matter of time plus finding a rich husband to pay the eventual upkeep.

Mrs. Fredley-Pugh was making a joke.

*Laugh.*

"I've already made my contribution to JOG," she grinned hideously with carmined lips. "I had my husband fire his pretty young secretary and hire a grandmother of 55."

They laughed, then controlled their mirth and moved on to serious talk. Tickets to the benefit were $25

25

each, tax deductible. Champagne punch and toothpaste sandwiches included.

Melissa swallowed a yawn. The same women whose names studded the society pages day after day, attending this benefit and that, tax deductible, would turn up at the Steuer Gallery wearing their newest dresses and jewels. Benefits kept haute couture alive. Where else could clothes be shown off to such good advantage and create the most jealousy?

They would pay their $25, drink the champagne, smile for the committee-paid photographer and completely ignore the paintings. Professional society people never bought works of art. They came to be seen, not to see.

After weeks of meetings, phone calls and frenetic rushing around, the net profits would go for printing leaflets urging big industries to support JOG. The leaflets would be mailed to personnel heads. Then the committee would consider its mission done and look for another segment of society that needed its help.

"If one grandma gets a job, I'll eat Mrs. Fredley-Pugh's hat," Melissa whispered.

"You'll die."

"Why do we *do* this to ourselves?"

"You know as well as I do," Ingrid answered, deadly serious. "Because we want to be insville looking out instead of outsville looking insville."

Glancing at Mrs. Rhinehart's outdated mink wrap and its obvious worn spots, Melissa said, "I think we have company. Mrs. Rhinehart is using the committee technique to marry off young Bettijane this season or die in the attempt. Did you hear that she worked in Milgrim's under an assumed name until one of her friends spotted her? She ducked behind a screen and quit that afternoon. Maybe they're living on unemployment insurance. Who knows?''

''I didn't hear that, but I did find out she's hired a press agent, some phony prince or other, to build Bettijane up as the Deb-Of-The-Year. Serving on committees gets their name in the paper and gives them a society label.''

''But how can they pay a press agent?'' Melissa murmured.

''Darling! I'm surprised at you, you child of nature. They make a deal and he gets a set fee when Bettijane either marries Mr. Big . . .''

''Like Philip Winston?''

''Like Philip . . . or gets a movie contract or a TV show or whatever. To be vulgar, he owns a piece of Bettijane.''

Melissa sighed in admiration. If only her own mother had been an organizer. How reassuring to have seasoned general, a Mama Gabor, in charge of maneuvers, someone to wheel and deal for you instead of having to do it yourself.

Ingrid had done it herself. A complete metamorphosis. Brown Mediterranean hair bleached Scandinavian white. Lyrical Anna Maria Francesca to cool, cool Ingrid. Crumbling brown tenement in the East Bronx to marble white town house on the East Side of Manhattan.

''With that blonde hair, who would ever believe you were Italian!'' Melissa had said soon after they became friends and secrets were shed. ''You *can't* be Italian. I've seen all those movies! Your nostrils don't flare!''

27

"And my breasts are too small."

"And you're too tall for Vittorio de Sica."

"For him, M'liss, I'd stoop a little. In fact, we could play our scenes lying down. *Maron*!" She had shaken a limp hand.

The official meeting over, ten minutes of girl-talk lay ahead, an unwritten formality of Committeeland. Mrs. Fredley-Pugh signalled her changeover from Chairman to Inquisitor by uncrossing her legs and re-crossing them the other way.

"And what have you been up to, Ingrid dear? We all saw you on *Vogue*. Exquisite, my dear, simply exquisite."

The queen recognizing the celeb.

"Thank you," Ingrid said, wearing her aloof $100-an-hour face. "Juni is rather a miraculous photographer, you know. He plays Chopin and sprays the studio with a heavy oriental scent. You just can't help being ethereal."

The other women, particularly Bettijane, were examining her now that they had an excuse, with a mixture of raw jealousy and acute interest. There but for lack of bone structure sat they.

"Nothing much else doing," Ingrid was saying, her audience intent. "I'm trying gradually to ease away from modelling, which believe it or not is very hard work and pretty boring after a while."

Incredulous breathing at the idea of relinquishing $100 an hour for standing like a stick and looking emaciated.

"What I want to do is something more constructive . . . more personally gratifying."

"You mean marriage?" Bettijane's mother asked

almost too quickly. She had had her gimlet eye on Philip Winston for her own offspring, fully aware of his onetime interest in Ingrid before Bernard Nahoum's star had risen, albeit a Star of David.

"No—not for a while yet," the girl colored. "I was taking about fashions. I've been having talks with a big buying office about setting up package tours of fashions which I would take out, like the road company of a Broadway show, to the biggest stores in the country."

"It's a marvellous idea," Melissa broke in by way of corroborative support.

"Of course, I don't work for the glory of it. I've asked for a whacking great fee and if they can't meet my price I won't go. Travelling is hard on a girl. Heels break. Baggage gets smashed. All these things have to be considered. And if they don't want to shell out, well then, Melissa and I are going into the Boutique business. Baubles, bangles, beads—fantastic scarves and bags and oddities of fashion you'll find nowhere but *nowhere* else." She was on a monologue and anxious to get off but nobody said anything.

"And when we have our opening, we'll run a benefit for JOG!" Melissa added.

The ladies twittered with mixed emotions.

The waiter arrived with the bill and, as was customary, each paid for her own refreshment. Another ten dollar bill shot to hell, Melissa thought. Helping grandma was expensive. Maybe someday she'd be a grandma looking for work and the grandchildren of these delightful ladies would form a subcommittee to help her. Whoopee! Psychiatrists said that most men suffered sexual fantasies about their mothers. Maybe

29

in fifteen or twenty years, our emotional growth as a nation would be such that she could start an Older Woman's Escort Service, providing mother figures for young men. Instead of running a string of ponies, these would be mares, or more lovingly to the point, nags. The House of the Rousing Son.

"I'll drop you home," Ingrid offered. "You've got that architect coming. He sure flipped for you, Missy. Did you see his face when we drove away?"

"Oh, Ingrid," Melissa grinned happily. "It wasn't me. It was you and the car and everything!"

This was the instinctual basis of their friendship. A genuine liking for each other was the tiny raisin at the core, covered over with generous gobs of reciprocal aid, comfort and charity. It was about as close a friendship as two healthy, ambitious females could have. Women, especially those who must depend solely on their own resources for survival, can never overcome an inherent suspicion of other creatures as a threat to security.

Melissa and Ingrid were enough the same and enough different to provide each other with a sounding board, honest opinion and a cheering section. Each felt it a duty to boost the other's ego, rejoice in the other's triumphs, mourn the other's grief. They were torn between being emancipated modern women with a realistic view of sex, morals and personal identity and becoming the pampered chattels of omnipotent leaders.

What Melissa really wanted, she had said one day when both were trying on chinchilla coats at a fur salon, was to be someone's chattel, but on her own terms.

Pleased and animated by Ingrid's compliment and the possibility of making Walter Simpson a new conquest, Melissa said, "Why don't you come in and have a drink with us?"

"Can't. Philip's picking me up at nine and I intend to spend the next few hours getting ready."

"Few hours! My God, Ingrid, it's only six now. For someone who can change in three minutes flat for the camera, why do you need three hours for Philip Winston?"

"Pride, girl," Ingrid smiled cruelly. "Pure Pagan pride. He better wear sunglasses because I am going to dazzle him. I'm going to drive him up the wall—subtly, of course!"

"Of course!" Melissa laughed. "Try a little Spanish Fly in the canapés!"

But her companion wasn't listening. She had mentally begun the pagan ritual. "First, I'm going to take all my clothes off, then I'm going to take all my makeup off. Then, I'm going to put my hair up in rollers and submerge the body up to the chin in that new body-firming goo Daniels sent over from Paris in the diplomatic pouch . . . I think I'll put on some Spanish guitar while I soak—it makes me feel kinda sexy and relaxed at the same time."

"And then?" her friend prompted.

"And then? Well, that's supposed to make me so smooth old Philip'll have a rough time getting a grip on me, so I may have to spend some time sandpapering a few spots to give him a handhold." She giggled. "And then? I'm going to lie down with my feet higher than my head with a facial masque to dissolve all the anxiety lines, especially after that meeting. And then

31

when I've peeled off the masque, I'm going to apply some soft-focus makeup—only good under artificial light, but wow! And of course I've got to paint my toenails and mix a few lethal martinis—''

"DON'T BRUISE THE GIN!" both girls shouted together.

"What are you going to wear?" Melissa asked.

"Jersey knit. Philip once told me it drives him wild when he sees girls' thighs outlined in fabric."

"Boy—you ought to get some thigh falsies, really let them protrude! You sure are doing some fancy plotting, Ingrid. I thought you'd given up on Philip."

Ingrid's voice turned metallic.

"I'll never give up as long as there's a remote chance of snaring him. Philip can give me everything I've dreamed of since I first read about Brenda Frazier and coming-out parties and seasons for doing this and being here and turning up there. He's the closest thing to aristocracy in America. Really preferable to the Nahoums. After all, they *are* Jews, and no matter how rich and cultured, it's not the same thing!"

"Maybe you should have come back from Europe with a title. That would have given you a social cachet."

"Titles! A dime a dozen! Who needs 'em? That year I spent with Dior, Lord rest him, I could have been the Marchioness of Munch-on-Crunch—the Comtessa di Whatsis—but who wants to live in a drafty castle? Nice strong, upright American men for me. Three cheers for the red, white and blue!"

"Well, don't sell yourself short," Melissa said staunchly.

32

"It's going to be interesting seeing how well Beauty can make out with the beast in Philip tonight!"

Fear and irony underscored her self-confidence. Most of Ingrid's juices were in her head. Love-making was pleasant, flattering, and a gratifying tribute to her loveliness. Sexual lust was always something she had pretended to feel, aping the expressions in books and films, convinced that this was the way things were—until she met Philip.

Sexual awakening had been a blessing and a curse. A blessing to find yourself capable of animal passion, yes, but a curse to find yourself its victim rather than its mistress. To reach your goal in life, you had to be ruthless. To win a man, he had to need you. You could admire him, adore him, enjoy his body, but never, by the slightest sign or neurotic compulsion, must you ever reveal your own passionate need for him.

Desire was a curse on the ambitious girl. It made her forget the Main Chance, and think only of the moment.

Walter Simpson was leaning against Melissa's door as they pulled up in front of the house. Rush-hour traffic squawked as Ingrid stopped to let Melissa out.

"Watch out for that T-Square!" she whispered, then screeched away in third gear before reaching the proper speed.

"That poor engine," Simpson cringed.

"Oh, it's all right," Melissa said, airily. "It's not hers."

His eyebrows bristled. "You and your girl friend may think it's all right, but an automobile is a delicate

33

mechanism, a balance of engineering skill and mechanical art. It should be respected."

My, my. If he felt that protective about cars, how about women?

"Oop. Sorry. My mistake," she said.

She fumbled with her door keys. "I can never find the right key or if I do I can't seem to get it to work. Drives me mad—sometimes I even kick the door if nobody's looking."

"Kick away. I won't tell. Good for the inhibitions. I'll join you." He kicked the door, a curiously juvenile action for a man with grey hair.

"Must have something to do with my psyche or something," she muttered, bent over the lock. "Hate locked doors; but you can't very well leave the front door open in the big bad city. A truck could pull up and cart away the whole household and nobody would say boo!"

"Here, let Big Walt take charge."

He took the key ring, inserted the first key, twisted the doorknob and quite easily opened the door.

"If you'll pardon the expression, I'm something of a lay analyst and I think I can tell you exactly what your problem is with keys and locks."

"Do I have to lie down on the couch?" she forced a laugh. He obviously used Little Racy Speeches as party patter.

"That would be nice but unnecessary—for our first consultation."

Doctor jokes made her yawn.

"All right, doctor. Let me have your diagnosis."

"Well, Mrs. Kempton—"

"Melissa is fine."

34

"Melissa—and you can call me Walt—You see, Melissa, our lives are guided by symbols. Mother symbols, father symbols, phallic symbols, sex symbols . . . tell me if I'm going too fast . . ."

"Oh no. I used to play the cymbals in the school band but I had weak ankles, had to give it up."

She took his hat and indicated a chair in the living room. He continued.

"Now, take your average lock and the keys that go into them. They are sex symbols."

"My God! And to think how careless I am with them."

Unperturbed, he pressed on. "The lock by its very design is a female sex symbol whereas the key itself, by the very nature of *its* design and *its* function in conjunction with the lock, is a male sex symbol."

"Oh—and when I think how I throw my keys around and lose them and abuse them and use them to pry open jars of olives and things. Oh . . ." She fluttered her eyelids incredulously.

"So you see your problem about opening doors is the normal healthy reaction of a normal healthy young female, resisting what is essentially a male act of penetration. It's your feminine aversion to the mere suggestion of a male function which fact alone makes you a unique specimen in modern day America. Tell me—have you ever been in analysis?"

"Why, no, Doc. Have you?"

"Well—no. Not that I haven't got problems," he hastily assured her, "but—well, I believe God put man on earth to help himself. And anyway I've read all the books on psychoanalysis . . . and I think I've come to terms with my hostilities and my inability to

35

relate in certain situations. So why pay a doctor when I can be my own doctor?''

"I'll buy that! Have a drink, doctor!''

"I never drink while on a case." *How many times had he said that*? "So I'll have scotch on one rock, please." *And that*! "But to get back to your case, Melissa, your symptoms are very sig-nif-icant, very sig-nif-icant indeed. What you need is—''

She held her breath, afraid to ask. He must be a riot at college reunions.

"—is a man around the house to take care of things like male symbols.''

She suddenly remembered the eviction. "Well, thanks to you and your friends, doctor, I won't be having that worry much longer. When you throw me out of here, I won't have a key *or* a lock to worry about.''

Confident his charm was working, he sipped his drink. "I knew we'd have to get down to business. Kind of hate to leave Dr. Walt.''

Candidly, his eyes examined the room, noting the wood-burning fireplace, the thick vermillion carpeting and the handsomely grouped water colors and Elizabethan prints fanning out from one enormous Swedish poster. Reflected in the mirror over the mantlepiece, they were the rough setting for the furniture whose period she defined as "Early Salvation Army.''

Each piece was old; not old enough to be an antique yet too unique to be stigmatized as second-hand. Melissa had spent weeks at the Salvation Army warehouse during her engagement to Max picking out item by item as replacements for the foam rubber gymnasium that had served his bachelorhood.

36

"I suppose you enjoy being the hatchet man for a bunch of speculators," she said peevishly. "They don't want this property for anything useful or really beautiful. They just want to play, like little boys with an erector set. 'What'll we build now and where?' . . . 'Ah, *here*'s a sweet little house and some nice little girl has gradually put it in shape so that it's comfortable and pleasant to live in.' *Pow*! They can't stand that! Buy the house. Throw the girl out. Send over Frankenstein with his T-square and let him create a new monster!"

She wrung her hands, the ageless gesture of frustration. 'When are you bringing around the big machine with the steel ball to knock all my walls in? Is that the sex symbol of the home-wrecker? What are you going to put up here—an aluminum cheesebox with one-room cells? Pullman kitchen and stall showers only! No room in the plans for tubs! Cut out the tubs. Let 'em take showers! Gets twelve more apartments. Progress!"

More distressed than she knew, she stormed on, "Back to the dawn of history. Back to the cave. 'Be a ferret and survive!' 'Elbow room,' cried Dan'l Boone!—that's what we need now, elbow room. In Daniel Boone's time, if you saw your neighbor's smoke on a clear day you knew it was time to move on. How do you think Dan'l Boone would have felt about one-room apartments?"

"From what I've read of his personal habits," he said, mildly, "he wouldn't need the stall shower at all. He could take in a boarder. Davey Crockett, maybe. Get rich that way, beyond his wildest dreams." This was a subject he knew. "It may interest you to know that the only reason Dan'l Boone went west in the first place is that he couldn't make out in the east. He scrawled his name on tree trunks as a trail in case anyone came looking for him to invite him back. Nobody ever did."

She had to laugh at his solemn face. "Maybe it's because he spelled bear 'bar' and they didn't want to fool with no alcoholic."

"Kee-rect. Andthat's how the west was settled." He leaned back and crossed his slim, well-tailored legs, one long, narrow foot tapping against the cocktail table.

"Forgive me for sounding off at you, Walter. Making you the heavy. It's just that I'm beside myself. I've done everything I know to stop the eviction proceedings." *Today's lunchless lunch the most desperate measure.* "I don't want to leave here. It's my home, the only place in this world that I feel is mine, where I feel safe. After my divorce a year ago I felt so rejected, so useless to anyone including myself that for the first time in my life I stopped caring. Screw 'em! Screw everybody and everything! I paid my two dollars but I didn't get my choice. I didn't get *anything.*"

She paced nervously. "So, while the outside of me continued to flourish like a hot-house nectarine, inside I shrivelled up—the traditional prune—hard, sour and only good for the more clinical functions. In the last year, my whole (admittedly superficial) life has revolved around this house. It's become the May Pole and every day's the first of May. This house is my anchor, my home base. I'm safe here. If you make me leave I'll become a nomad, one of those forever-

38

smiling homeless ones who live in residential hotels or share too-small apartments with other girls and lose every vestige of privacy. Well, I can't go back to that!"

She stood over him, accusingly. "I'm twenty-eight years old and I have been married. Spaghetti dinners on the floor of a raunchy Greenwich Village walkup are part of my childhood. I can't go back to being somebody's roommate, fighting over who drank the Scotch and who hides out in the movies while the other rolls in the hay!"

"You make it sound pretty bad, except that as a lecherous married man, I kinda go for gals who cook me a spaghetti dinner in Greenwich Village or anywhere else. I even bring them wine and flowers. But—" he said, pulling her down beside him, "—if my being the heavy makes you feel any better, okay, only it doesn't really help you. Just listening to you—and here I go again as your friendly neighborhood head-shrinker—I would say the villain is this house. This deceptively warm, friendly, safe little house has given you a false security that deep inside you don't really accept. Yet you cling to it, afraid to leave, afraid of being alone outside in the big, bad world."

"You make the house sound like a mother," she said dreamily. One gin made her dreamy. "And I'm the unborn baby afraid to come out. Wow!" She fell back against the cushions, sloshing her drink. "What a gin does for my preoccupation with Mom! Now you're making my house a mother figure."

"You'd be surprised. There's a womb-like quality to many homes, from one room apartments to man-

39

sions. As an architect, I'm like the iceman, on intimate terms with the ways hundreds of people live. Some make dark, warm, damp caverns of the brightest rooms, covering the windows with heavy drapes, sealing them so no fresh air comes in, only a kind of moist ventilation pumped in through tubes and porous vents."

"I always have the windows open!" She shot back defensively. "Even in the winter!"

He grinned. "Don't take me so literally, Melissa. As I said, I'm the original drawing room analyst."

The phone.

Always the phone.

"Uh-oh, Groupsville! You've been so fascinating, Walter, I forgot to check my service."

Her answering service operator had several messages. A Mr. Butler had called about a free-lance job and wanted her to call him in the morning. Calvin Burns called, would try again. Dominic Minto wished to have dinner with her but was having drinks first at 21 and would check back later. David Pelham was dining with friends on their yacht moored at the 79th Street basin but would like to meet afterwards and would check back as to where. Judie and Julian were making up a poker party if she wanted to sit in.

Groupsville was like that. The loosely knit collection of friends and acquaintances running as fast as their chic legs could carry them on individual moving platforms, grouping together at rendezvous points to exchange gossip and lovers, moving erratically on as if run by a carny man's switch only to regroup again and again in overlapping orbits of social and business enterprise.

40

Members of Groupsville adhered to certain regulations, chief of which was "checking." At some time during the day, every day, members would call each other and divulge their plans or lack of same for the evening ahead. Tentative arrangements for meeting were discussed and affirmed. This was done with complete sincerity even though everyone concerned knew the plans would probably be changed. As evening approached, new rendezvous points were communicated along the line. That is, David Pelham would tell Ingrid that he was having a nightcap at Michael's Pub at midnight and she and Bernard should try to get hold of Melissa and Dominic and whoever else was free.

Naturally, on arrival at Michael's, there would be other messages waiting—David is late, wants them to join him at Goldie's or check his answering service for word on exactly where he will be. The epitome of Groupsville living was to avoid actual verbal contact and leave all negotiations to the answering services. "My answering service will leave a message with your answering service . . ." etc.

Groupsville plus answering service combined all the elements of an endless scavenger hunt with the players chasing down clues, switching partners, catching up with their team in the race against (and inevitably toward) boredom.

Groupsville International was a subsidiary element, concerned mainly with departures and arrivals and reciprocal acceptance in other cities. Johnny might fly in from London, Teretsky from the coast, Enrico and Suzie from Rome. They, too, must have people with whom to check later and catch up. In return, they provided the same service for visitors in their home territory. Membership lapsed when the need to mingle with many was eclipsed by a satisfaction with one.

Melissa made squiggly notes of her messages, a curious warmth suffusing her body with the solace of a familiar narcotic. She was a mainliner. She *needed* her daily dosage of messages and meetings. She *needed* her answering service and its assurance of someone answering her phone when she was out. Reading them all, there was not one concrete invitation except for Dominic and dinner. But with Dominic, dinner might be 11:30, or never. That was one of the risks of Groupsville. No dinner.

Walter Simpson seemed impressed by the whole thing. He hadn't suggested dinner yet, though. She was hungry. The only thing to eat in the kitchen was a jar of liver paté, a can of Chinese noodles and, of course, the peanut butter.

"Sounds like quite a service you have there," he remarked. "I hadn't realized it was used as a social secretary. I thought it was mainly for—" he was going to say call girls, changed his mind "—young lawyers who can't afford a secretary and actress types who, uh, have to be available—that is—to producers—"

This time she was defensive and indignant, too. "It's not purely social! It's a professional necessity!" That's what her income tax return stated emphatically. "I do free-lance work—fashion commentating, interior decorating, other things. I have to be in touch all the time or I might lose out on a job."

"Is that what you were doing this afternoon with your friend? She's a model, isn't she?"

A spasm of jealousy cut her answer with a cool disdain. "That was Ingrid Gaard, one of the highest paid fashion models in the world and we were on our way to a committee meeting at the Plaza—"

"—the highest-priced hotel in the world. It follows."

"—to plan a charity benefit," she finished with a pompous sniff.

"We-ell . . . Lady Astor! What's the charity? Mink coats for French poodles?"

She giggled despite herself. "No—Jobs for Grandmothers." At which they both burst out laughing.

*Ask me to dinner, you clown,* she urged silently as they grinned at each other. *Come on, Walter! Baby is hungry and almost homeless. Ask her to dinner!*

He not only took showers, but his underwear was immaculate, she was sure.

"Club women!" he exploded mirthfully. "The great American substitute. Don't live, convene! Every time I read about this club and that club, this committee and that committee sticking their faces into this or that situation, all I can think of is, somebody, somewhere isn't getting enough . . ."

He tapped his foot reflectively.

"Isn't getting enough what?" she demanded. She knew.

"Isn't getting enough!" he said with broad sarcasm. "Everybody's doing everything but nobody's getting enough! The men aren't getting enough because they don't know how and because they think they're animals to want what they want and the women aren't smart enough to know what the men want so the women aren't getting enough either, and they don't know what the hell to do. Result? Everybody joins things and does things and avoids facing the facts."

43

"But committees and clubs do things, accomplish things. Take care of unwed mothers, raise money for mental health and heart research . . ."

"If everybody was getting enough there wouldn't be any tensions and, *ipso facto*, no heart disease, no mental breakdowns. Instead of joining together for the good of the community they ought to spend that time in bed gratifying themselves and their mates and putting the whole community in a happy frame of mind. Or, if the herd instinct is strong, they should meet and read essays on My Most Satisfactory Sexual Experience and listen to lectures on—"

The phone again.

Thank God!

"Melissa darling! Is it really you?"

Horray! Dinner! Walter had become downright incendiary.

"Martin. How nice." Bette Davis on a binge.

The flat New England voice exclaimed with pleasure. "You recognized my voice. How clever you are. I thought you were going to be that sassy operator again, the one who treats your host of admirers as if they were dirt."

"No, it's just little old me. How are things with the club car set? Are you still battling the New Haven or have you organized your own railroad?"

"Oh, it's still the same old rat race. I pay off the mortgage with my bridge winnings. With that and the tips on the market I get every morning, I can retire from business forever. But the most important thing on my mind right now is, how are you? What unspeakable mischief have you been up to, my amber-eyed vixen? What wild adventures?"

"Oh, just the usual quiet life." She smiled at Walter. "El Morocco, the Colony, 21, 22, 23, 24 . . . same old jazz. All men look alike in black ties. *You* know . . ."

"Ah, yes, but all too infrequently." She was his link with notoriety. "Tell me, my dear, how do you look? I haven't seen you in months. What are you wearing? Are you lying on your bed talking to me?"

Martin was what she called an *ecouteur*, as opposed to a *voyeur*. That is, he liked to *listen* to descriptions of clothes. Maybe his own imagination served him better than any reality. He always asked her what she was wearing.

Winking at Walter she said, "I'm swathed in a red negligee of Oriental silk and I'm stretched out on my chaise longue, munching Indian nuts and reading Baudelaire aloud in the original to a business associate of mine who is stretched out on the floor at my feet."

"You're impossible, darling. Breathtakingly impossible. I can just see you—I *want* to see you—in fact that's why I'm calling at this outrageously late hour to find out if just by chance, by the merest good luck, you can dine with me tonight. I've reserved the largest steak in New York in the hope you would do me that honor."

Dinner!

"What keeps you in town?" she stalled. "Did you miss your train?"

"Melissa! You're too cruel. The most glamorous creature in my humdrum life and she's heartless. There was supposed to be a meeting tonight with our Texas affiliate but he caught some bug or other—"

"Hoof and mouth disease?" she asked sweetly.

45

"More than likely!" he chortled. "And he's tucked away at the Waldorf, ten-gallon hat and all. I'm not expected home until the midnight train and I would like nothing better than to see you. There. You've wrung a confession from me."

"Well—" (Dinner at last!) "—I was going to meet some dreary friends later on but I do think dinner with you would be more fun." She paused again to prolong the suspense. "Come pick me up in half an hour."

Walter examined his watch with prolonged attention as if it were an Ethiopian sundial. "Hey, there! Seven-thirty. Must run. There's a small matter of a small redhead—a singer at the Copa. She finishes her dancing lesson at eight and she's letting me buy her dinner."

"I see," she said, disappointed at not being able to fling him out into the friendless night. "One more before you go? We really didn't begin to talk about the house."

A red-haired Copa girl! Adolescents Anonymous. Walter obviously wasn't getting enough, either.

"No thanks. Sorry I can't stay. Redheads are delicate creatures, you know. They wilt if you're late." His boyish eagerness about the redhead both touched and outraged her with renewed jealousy. "But I do want to go through the house if you can stand having me do it. How about the early part of the week? Would that be convenient?"

Standing close beside her at the door, he said, "This is a professional visit and I don't care how long it drags on." He was the football captain trying to have every girl in the school. "Do you?"

46

"For my part, you can come every day for the next twenty years so long as I stay here!"

"Goodbye, Melissa. I kind of hate to leave you here all by yourself in this house, though from the way your phone rings I guess you're not *too* lonely."

From anyone else, it might have been a compliment. From him it was a dirty crack.

"On your way out, don't slam the door!" she said. "And watch out for the grating near the door. It's loose."

"Why don't you have it fixed?"

"That's for the owner to do. You forget. *I'm* being evicted!"

The door slammed followed by the clang of metal and a series of robust remarks.

She opened the window. "Hurt yourself?"

"Oh no—just broke my leg."

He limped toward the corner.

"By-ye . . . Have a good t-ime!" she sang after him, mentally computing the number of scotches he had consumed and translating the amount into hard cash. A good investment nonetheless. He might, just might help her to stay here. He liked her, she could tell. Redhead or no redhead.

Martin Blake was a prick-tease. His own, that is. In fantasy he was the sophisticated executive with a solid family life centered on a Connecticut household of half-grown progeny to carry on his name and a secret city life centered on a little black book filled with the names of slightly older progeny who were ready to jump on the carousel with him at a moment's notice.

In actuality, the black book was a loose-leaf affair.

47

Inactivated pages were crumpled mercilessly and thrown away. He kept the book well filled so that when the mood hit him he could always count on finding somebody free for the evening, even if it meant an hour on the phone. He kept a supply of perfume in his office so as to always have a little "gift" for his dinner partner (a gallant touch, he felt) and an extra shirt in his attaché case for a quick change in case of an inept lipstick smudge. (Indelible lipstick *does* rub off girls, does *not* come off shirts.)

He lived by two rules unto himself. He never tried to take his companions to bed, although he could be a bore in a taxi. And he never made dates in advance, part of the reason being his fantasy of impromptu adventure, the real reason being self-justification. Nobody could ever say he was *really* cheating his wife since he didn't go in for pre-planned clandestine meetings. Dinner out with a girl mostly "just happened" because he "just happened" to be delayed in town. Also, of perverse importance to him was his extra-marital celibacy. A man can't be unfaithful if he doesn't top them, can he?

Above all, he held himself socially superior to the young women like Melissa who were not protected by family even though he in effect preyed on them, the actresses and secretaries and models who bubbled with gaiety and vigor from a wellspring of youth. In spite of his position as head of the largest industrial film company in the east, he never raised a finger to help any of them, Melissa included, with their careers. No refused to be involved, however refreshing it might be to his ego.

"How's your love life?" he asked, an avuncular

hand on Melissa's thigh. This was a question that irritated her to the extreme yet Martin never failed to ask it. Completely out of character for him, it signified his temporary tryst with the demi-monde.

"Thriving," she said with a trace of mockery. "How's yours?"

Martin's physical appearance was a monochrome. Dark gray suit, paler gray tie, paler yet gray eyes set like a half-tone photograph of fried eggs in the grayish pallor of a boyish face. Graying blonde hair trimmed in an almost-bald crewcut revealed an opaque dandruff-free scalp.

His hands and fingernails were antiseptic gray-white, like a male nurse's after years of scrubbing up and scrubbing down. His mouth and earlobes were waxy white, totally drained of color as if by a malicious chapstick.

Slim, brisk, direct, he looked terribly Class of '31, Small New England College, emotionally suspended between Scott Fitzgerald abandon and upper middle class diligence.

"Nothing interesting ever happens to me," he said. "It's you who lead the gay life and I live vicariously through you!" He believed what he said.

"Well," she smiled, "let me tell you how gay it's been lately. I'm being evicted. The landlord sold out and they want me to leave so the law's after me—"

"Oh, how sad . . . this lovely little house . . . and you a fugitive from justice?"

"Yep—the sheriff's after me. And let's see. What else? Oh, yes, I'm being wildly unsuccessful as a free-lance. Nobody wants me some of the time. So I'm flat broke, except for what Max sends me, of course."

49

"And for a girl of your tastes that won't go very far, will it?"

"No, I guess not. The trouble is I was born too late. I'm just a dilettante. I paint. I do ceramics—you've seen my little kiln in the basement—and I design clothes and run fashion shows—"

"We're doing some industrial films with a fashion angle. Maybe we can work you in as a commentator. Let me speak to the producer."

He wouldn't speak to him and he wouldn't take the chance of mixing business with pleasure. She had been up this garden path before and all she'd gotten was rocks in her shoes. Rocks in her head for ever taking him seriously.

"That's sweet of you, Martin," she said, her hand tightly pressed on his hand to prevent its moving. "But right now, I'm hungry. Feed me, Martin. At once!"

He loved being ordered around, a fact his business associates (fortunately for him) did not perceive.

"At your command, Princess. I've booked a corner table at the Steak Club so we can be comfortable."

And unobserved. She knew how his mind worked.

"Before we go, I have a little present for you." He opened his attaché case. There, nestled in the collar of the clean just-in-case shirt was a white box.

"Oh, Martin. How sweet of you to remember! Crêpe de Chine. My favorite scent. And as usual, I'm on the brink of running out."

"You can wear it with that red negligée you had on when I telephoned.

"Oh, Martin!" she laughed. "Martin, I'm sorry. I made that up. I don't own a red negligee. It just seemed . . . well, I just felt when I heard your voice that I *should* be wearing a red negligee!''

He extracted a new hundred dollar bill from his money clip just slowly enough for her to glimpse its denomination and folded it under the tab of the Crêpe de Chine package. ''No girl with your hair and figure and vivacious coloring should be without a red negligée. Please allow me the pleasure of buying it for you. The next time I call, you won't have to make up fibs.''

She knew that *he* knew that *she* knew that he was playing Diamond Jim Brady and did not expect her to buy the negligée or if she did, to pay a quarter the price.

''You make me feel wicked—and loved,'' she solemnly kissed his cheek, taking the package from him.

How nice that he was handing out hundred dollar bills tonight! When you don't know what to give, give money.

She thought of Dominic. He might call while she was out, expecting her to join him. Well, this time let him be nervous and waiting. She left no message for him with the answering service.

''Oohhhhhh, it's pure ecstacy! I can hardly bear it,'' she moaned a while later, arching her back and closing her eyes, her mouth working in a slow, dreamy rhythm. ''The best steak I've ever had! Too much. Can't eat another bite.''

''Nor can I,'' Martin said. ''Seems a pity to leave it but they do tend to overdo the hospitality here.''

''Leave it?'' she asked incredulously. ''Not on your life.'' She beckoned the waiter. ''Would you mind wrapping these leftovers for my dog?''

The waiter gone, she turned to Martin, her hands drooping paw-like at her chest. *Rrrrrr . . . uffffffff!*''

Still later, drinking brandies at a quiet bar near Grand Central, a piano thumping show tunes in the background, Melissa was bored. An hour with Martin was quite enough. How did the professional party girls do it night after night, being gay and charming with dull, rich men?

Sleeping with them was the easiest part, she concluded, although she was glad Martin's inhibitions precluded that problem.

How many more pointless evenings would she have to endure before finding someone whose instincts and needs matched her own? Staying home alone was even worse than these abortive forays into society where something, some tantalizing miracle, some happenstance was always on the verge of changing her life.

The shadow man she wanted to find her would be looking for a woman figure, not a mother figure to revere or a whore figure to degrade. Men wanted her, but never in the way she wanted to be wanted. They lusted for her luxuriant breasts which were supposed to be an asset in this, The Mammary Age, but instinct warned her that a man's delight turned to disgust with a figure that was too ripe, too lush, too overwhelmingly a mother configuration, full to bursting with nutriment. It confused and frightened them. Being a woman frightened them; being a mother frightened *her*.

And as Ingrid so wisely said, they were getting old. The marriage prizes went to the young and fair, or even the young and unfair. Ingrid's goal was clearcut. She wanted high society more than anything and could adjust her passions accordingly. Melissa liked the idea of high society if she didn't have to work too hard at it. Her love image swam hazily in her mind. She was shopping with "I'll know it if I see it" uncertainty.

But would she know it? Or give it the fish eye? Or choose wrong again like Max? Oh, Max . . . why couldn't you have grown up and been the man I wanted? Why couldn't you be a man! Why did you let your mother destroy us? Make us do something we never should have . . .

Brandy brought on the weeps.

Fortunately it was dark. Not that Martin would notice or want to notice tears. He was describing in detail the complexities of his golf score the previous weekend when by judicious overshooting he had captured a new contract for a series of training films.

"Martin . . ." she interrupted. "What time is your train?"

"Midnight, little witch. Midnight, Cincerella . . ."

"Well, it's 11:30. Shouldn't we be pressing off stationward?"

"So soon? Pumpkin time so soon, Cinderella? Say it's not so soon, M'liss. Let's turn back the clocks. It's Greenwich *Mean* time, all right, all right. Let's get some Mountain *Pleasant* time. We're having a pleasant time, aren't we? I dowannagohome!"

"Martin!" Emergencies cleared her head. "The Midnight is the last train to Darien, isn't it? You have to be on it."

"Why can't I stay at my club?"

"No. You're expected home." She was tired because she was bored. The thought of pub-crawling for several more hours strengthened her determination to speed him on his way. Still, she must be polite, at least a hundred dollars worth.

"I know . . ." she said with sudden inspiration. "Quick . . . Let's get a cold bottle of champagne and two glasses. We can drink it as a nightcap in a taxi up to 125th Street. I'll put you on the train there! Shee you off with champagne! How chic can you be? No other commuter has ever had the champagne treatment. Come on! We can just make it."

The idea thrilled Martin, made him feel like a playboy being seen off on a safari with a pretty girl in one hand and a bottle of Mumm's in the other instead of a middle-aged executive on his way to exurbia with an attaché case full of laundry.

Up Park Avenue they raced, toasting the elegant buildings and their unknowing doormen as they passed. "Here's good luck to 720 Park. Down the hatch!" "And cheers to the doorman at 1060 . . ." At 96th Street, the railroad tracks, under them all the while, came to the surface. No sign of a northbound train. It was 12:04 when they reached the 125th Street station.

"We made it, Martin!" she shouted exuberantly. "Now get up those stairs!"

"No—no—I've got a better idea," he said excitedly, gulping down his glass of bubbly. "The train stops at New Rochelle, too. We've got a head start. The damn thing's always late anyhow. Let's race it there! We haven't finished the bottle and I'm having too good a time!"

"BUT New Rochelle is miles away!" she protested.

"Never mind, my girl. Mere details. We have wings and a cool, competent pilot. To New Rochelle, driver!

54

And don't spare the horse power! The short, picturesque way if you please. Would you care for some champagne?''

"No thanks, Mac. Never touch the stuff since my kid's bar mitzvah. Gives me heartburn."

This started the driver off on a dissertation on digestion, his own. Without pause, he revealed to them, as if for the first time, the unique reaction of his gastric juices to all manner of liquids and solids. Across 125th Street. Up the West Side Drive. Through the mists of suburbia to the New Rochelle railroad station.

"Bacchanalian heaven," Martin murmured, sloshing the last of the champagne on Melissa. "Thank you for the most wonderful evening of my life, Melissa."

Bruied from the wild ride and Martin's elbows that knifed her every time the cab swerved, Melissa smiled weakly.

The train could be heard in the distance. He was getting on this train if she had to fling herself in front of it.

"Hey—I got an idea," Martin said.

"No—no—no, whatever it is, I don't want to hear it. Have a good trip home, Martin. See you soon."

He waved from his seat in the train, like an English film hero, a happy man.

"I could use some coffee," she said to the driver. "How about you?"

It was the wrong question. "It gives me heartburn," he said, beginning the recitation again.

"Okay, okay. Back to New York. El Morocco, please." Someone was bound to be there. "On second thought, make it East 50th Street." She was tired.

Dominic and the rest of Groupsville could drop dead. She was going to bed.

In retrospect, it had been a good evening. Martin had slipped her another fifty to pay the cabbie, who asked for only twenty-five. Feeling generous, she tipped him ten dollars, leaving a hundred fifteen profit plus the perfume plus the leftover cold steak. The only deficit was the champagne stain on her dress which meant a two dollar cleaning tab. The four hours of her time on earth she reckoned for a fleeting instant and dismissed.

Folded up on her doorstep was Calvin Burns, fast asleep, his smooth face looking younger than his twenty-five years, his moist pink mouth open and snoring, his arms cradling a rolled-up topcoat for a pillow.

"Calvin . . ." He started at her voice and slowly uncoiled his six feet three inches of flexibility.

"Hi, Melissa. I was waiting for you. Must have fallen asleep. So mild out tonight." He clutched her hand. "But I just had to see you. Desperately need your advice."

*Here we go again.*

"Calvin, honey, be a darling and go home. I'm pooped. It's late. After one. Can't it wait unti tomorrow?"

"M'liss, please. It's very important. I have to talk to you. There's nobody else I can go to. Please? I'll only stay a minute."

She was fiddling with the key in the lock, suddenly remembered Walter and his pocket psychoanalysis. "Here, Calvin! You open the door. It's so dark. Oh,

56

and be careful of that grating, hon. It's loose. Somebody fell over it once today already.''

"I won't stay but a minute. Promise." He followed her inside. "I won't even sit down."

"Sit down."

"All right. I'll sit down but I won't stay."

"Okay. Now, what's the problem?"

*You are old, Mother Melissa, the young man said. And your head is exceedingly light . . .*

Only a few years younger than she, Calvin made her feel ancient and wise, the Mother of them all. He was a member of what she called The Unsex, the borderline boys whose indecisive genitalia were reflected in a general vacillation of drives and a weakness of conviction.

The Unsex was only a little more exclusive a club than Groupsville, its members suspended in a high-compression purgatory with unlocked doors at both ends leading up or down according to choice.

Calvin also held charter membership in another club, Melissa's Stable, her collection of superficially attractive young men kept in tow for filling in at parties and as escorts when needed. For something like the JOG benefit at the Steuer Galleries that would irritate a Dominic or a Max, or even a Walter, beyond endurance, Calvin would leap at the chance to put on a black tie. He actually enjoyed being charming and helpful to guests and committee alike during the tedious proceedings.

Having a stable was an absolute necessity to the bachelor girl, she had discovered. One thing marriage gave you was an escort service, a benefit she had overlooked until her new-found freedom exposed the problems of digging up a date at short notice. Calvin had come to the rescue often and became Old Reliable. What Melissa appreciated most was he liked to wear a black tie, the traditional foible of the chest-beaters.

For complete social protection, she kept the stable large and active, rotating them as needed. Sometimes she arrived at parties with two escorts—young actors, writers, painters, dress designers like Calvin—boys who were socially gregarious and to whom it was understood you owed no allegiance once at your destination.

It was further understood that Melissa could dump the stable at a party and leave with somebody else with no hard feelings. They were a mixture of older brother and society mom combined. Unlike Max and some others she could name, they did not require looking after at parties or rescuing from untenable traps.

Calvin was her most loyal, most devoted and, unsurprisingly, her favorite.

"Quentin's flipped again. He locked up my clothes and says he won't let me move out! Just because he took me in when I didn't have any place to live doesn't mean he owns me, does it? Well, does it, Melissa? I walked out. O-U-T. Out. He can keep my things! They're charged to him anyhow. What's really bugging him is that I'm going into business for myself. He can't stand it. He accused me of using him, learning everything I could about couture from him and that I'm an ungrateful bastard!"

He bit a cuticle. She waited.

"So I'm an ungrateful bastard! So what the hell do I do, Melissa? I *am* grateful to Quentin. He's been like a *father* to me . . . well, you know what I

58

mean . . . but, hell, he practically wants to take away my shoes and chain me to the furniture when he isn't there. Christ! I've got to get out!''

With quiet compassion she said, ''Yes, you do have to get out, Calvin, and I'm glad you realize it. Quentin is a sweet, talented guy, but he's warped in a sense, all twisted up inside. He wants to own you. Do you know he doesn't speak to me anymore? He snubs me when we meet on the street. And why? Because I ask you to take me to parties or sit in on a poker game and he thinks I'm trying to take you away from him.''

''Oh, my God! That's just it! I *don't* belong to him! I don't belong to anybody! Hell! I don't even belong to myself. What am I going to do? I've got this new place all set. I can live and work in two of the rooms and fix the other one up for clientele—all the fittings stuff, swatch pads, everything! I'm doing the papering and painting myself. Everything's set! My dream come true, thank God for Cora Winchester and her money. Quentin's even threatened to talk her out of being my backer, to tell her I'm a cheat and a liar and unreliable and a lousy designer besides!''

He was almost in tears.

''Cora Winchester knows what she wants, Calvin. She's seventy if she's a day even with that junior miss figure. Her two interests in life are wearing a different dress to El Morocco every night and playing Goddess to talented and handsome young men, which is you on both counts.''

''Quentin says he knows her for years and he'll tell her the designs of mine she liked were really his! My God! This was my chance to get out, my chance to be something by myself. First it was my lousy stepfather running things and when I sprang from that jail, I fell flat on my ass. I couldn't make it. Then Quentin. *San* Quentin, I called him tonight and he threw a lamp at me. Jesus Christ—another, warden! I have to get out and maybe this time get some self-respect!''

Melissa had long ago learned that giving advice was nine-tenths listening, one-tenth soothing.

"Why don't you call Cora tomorrow and go to see her? She likes you. She obviously wants to help you to get started. Tell her frankly that Quentin is upset, maybe even a little jealous. After all, he's a designer, too.''

"Yes, but he specializes in sportswear. I won't be cutting in on his business. In fact we'd be sending custom to each other. Maybe you're right. Cora really seems to like me,'' he said wistfully.

"Women do like you, Calvin. You're a very sweet, appealing boy.''

*You are old, Mother Melissa . . .*

"Oh, M'liss. It's so much more than my own business. More than just getting away from Quent . . . You may not believe this, but I want to get married. I mean really married to a girl—a self-sufficient, independent girl like you, Melissa. I'll admit I don't have any real sex drive, but neither do I want to be a Goddam fag. I'm not a lisper! A mincer! A swisher. Jesus God, I'm no bitch, Melissa, and when I think of the last year, I could kill myself sometimes, taking the easiest way out for a lousy roof over my head!''

"You have a lot to give a woman, Calvin, particularly a woman who isn't too sexy herself. And, believe me, there are plenty of women who look on sex

60

as an accommodation. You're warm, and affectionate, and good company . . . intelligent . . . loyal . . ."

"—you make me sound like an Eagle Scout—" (obviously pleased.)

". . . and what's more you have good taste. Your wife would be the best-dressed gal in New York. I may marry you myself."

"Do you mean that?" he said, eyes intent.

"Oh, Calvin! I divorced one man for worshipping a mother figure and trying to make me over in her image. I'm too primitive for you, darling, but thanks anyway. The only honest offer I've had today."

He yawned, the full-throated yawn of a child who's been crying and is now quiet and ready for sleep.

"I feel better," he said. "If I know Quentin, he's locked me out, put the chain on the door, for spite. He wants me to ring the bell and beg to be let in. Well, screw him! I'll sleep in the park if I have to."

"Don't be stupid. They'll arrest you for vagrancy."

"Well," he pouted, "I'm not going back there."

"Okay. Okay. I give up. You can sleep down here on the couch."

A little while later she came down to tuck him in. At least someone needed her. Maybe she should marry him and make him a success and keep lovers on the side? No, that would be another descent in the escalator life of Melissa Kempton. She didn't want to catch her heel on another step.

"Feeling better, Calvin?" she murmured, making the blanket secure under the sofa cushions. "What's that you've got?"

"Oh, it's that ceramic figure you made, the one of a girl. I like the way it feels."

She took it from him. "You're a little old for sleeping with dolls. This was my first ceramic. Max didn't like it much but I do. Maybe it made him feel guilty."

"Why?"

"Never mind. It's too long and sad a story for now and besides, it's nearly two o'clock."

"After my business gets going, I'll open a boutique, too, and sell your ceramics, huh?"

"That'll be peachy keen, m'sieur. See you in the ayem." She kissed him on the forehead and turned out the lights.

"Hey, M'liss?"

"Yes, Calvin."

She half expected him to ask for a drink of water or a bedtime story.

"Hey—do you mind leaving on one light?" An embarrassed voice in the dark. "I—uh—I might wake up and forget where I am and break something."

She switched on a small table lamp in the far corner of the room.

"Okay? Night-night, sweetie. Don't worry now."

She opened her bedroom window and watered the plants on the tiny balcony. Two o'clock in the morning was some time to be watering plants. She didn't think the plants minded unless it made a difference to the chlorophyll process to water them when the sun was down. Still, rain fell at night so it couldn't hurt them.

Flopping into bed, she wondered if Groupsville had tried to find her. She dialled the answering service. Groupsville had not let her down. Rather, she had let them down by not being available. At ten, Dominic had called to say they were dining at Michael's Pub, at eleven he had called again. They were just starting dinner. At twelve, he left word for her to join them for coffee and brandy. Aha, she felt triumphant, let him wait. Retaliation for the many evenings she had been naive enough to turn up at rendezvous points on time, primly expecting to eat or do whatever the original plan called for. Groupsville wasn't like that. It operated on a glorified Army policy of check, meet, wait, check, meet, hurry up and wait.

She was dreaming of a nervous, pacing Dominic when the phone blasted her awake. She had forgotten to turn the gizmo to low. It was Dominic, waiting.

"Darling . . . I've been trying to find you for hours, simply hours. Where the hell did you disappear to? I was about to ring up the local constabulary, have them drag the river. Wherever were you, my poppet? But never mind. I've found you. Now put yourself into a taxi at once. I'm waiting for you at the bar. Morocco is dead, tonight, absolutely cadaverous. Not a single fight."

"Dominic, will you shut up for a minute? I am in bed, Dominic, asleep. Too much champagne. I was with an industrial film tycoon who may give me a job. Business, you know."

"Dammit, Melissa, I'm in the film business, too, so you must come because I may give you a job."

"But what time is it, Dominic? Isn't Morocco closed?"

"Another hour to go, poppet. It's just three and if you hurry we can dance for fully half an hour."

"But are you alone? What happened to everyone else?" Groupsville generally clung together in the wee hours.

"The group's deserted, paired off two by two running ahead of the flood, leaving me all by myself with a brandy.''

Melissa hesitated. She hated to pass up anything. It might never come again, including second helpings of chocolate sauce, parties when she really wanted to read, weekends with people who bored her.

Fatigue made the decision. ''No, Dominic. I can't. I'm beat and it would take me too long to dress. In addition to which I'm all neatly stashed away in bed and recovering my youth and beauty.''

''Please, poppet? For me?'' he cajoled. He was lonely and hated going back to his hotel. Soon this bloody TV film would be finished and he could go back to London. America depressed and unnerved him. Practically everything since the war did. There was simply no room for an Englishman of exemplary taste and breeding in the postwar world, particularly when the British film industry had become virtually non-existent and one had to compromise with that bastard cinema form, television. The Angry Young Men had inherited the earth. By their standards, he was middle-aged.

''No, darling. I've decided. Firmly. No. Though it breaks my heart. See you tomorrow? Let's check.''

''Now you mustn't put me off. I want to see you *now*. Or—'' his voice changed ''—aren't you alone?''

Calvin *was* downstairs, but he didn't exactly count. ''If I weren't alone do you think I would even answer the phone or talk so long? Of course I'm alone and faithful forever to you.''

''Well, then, I'll come there. What do you want? Brandy? A split of wine? Roast beef sandwich?''

''*Nothing*, Dominic, nothing and that includes you!

I'm going to sleep! Now! And I'm not interested in anything but sleep. And if you come I won't answer the door. You'll look mighty foolish standing on the street in the middle of the night. And—'' she searched for further argument ''—there's a grate come loose just outside the door. A man trap, all triggered to ambush night raiders.''

"All right, my darling. I'll check with you in the morning. See about plans for the day. I'm filming at some wretched studio in Brooklyn but only for an hour around tea time. Maybe you'll nip out there with me.''

"Love to. Goodnight.''

Working her body into the pliant hardness of the mattress, she lay on her back spread-eagled, wriggling her toes as she stretched, abandoning herself to the firm support beneath her back and buttocks and shoulders, the pillow a cool arm under her neck. Sometimes it was unbelievably good to be alone in a big bed.

The next time she awoke it was not to the phone but the insistence of a warm mouth and a hard tongue darting back and forth between her lips.

My God! *Calvin*? A kiss burglar?

She struggled in the embrace.

"Melissa . . .''

"DOMINIC! You idiot!'' She reached up and turned on the lamp. "How did you get in?''

"Through the balcony à la Fairbanks the Elder.'' He was obviously pleased with himself.

"But the wall? It must be fifteen feet!''

"You forget. I was a commando in His Majesty's 104th!'' He clicked his heels. "Small men, but agile!''

She laughed.

"Brandy puts springs in one's legs,'' he said modestly. "Don't be cross with me. I couldn't bear not to see you. I peered in the sitting room window right into the sleeping face of an exquisite young man. You didn't tell me you were running an orphanage."

"That's Calvin. He ran away from home. I'm playing Mom tonight."

"He looked so sweet I couldn't quite decide which of you I want more."

"Dominic, you're evil! And I've just remembered, I'm sleepy and angry. Go away! Or, as we say in Ameddica, get your dead ass out of here."

She pulled the covers over her head.

"My ass is far from dead as you shall discover presently," he announced with a trace of coldness, yanking the covers off her.

"Ah, what a shame—no frilly night dress to rip off your delicious body. All ready and waiting for me, isn't it, my dear Melissa? All its smoothness and roundness waiting to be bruised and flattened, all of the bubbles straining to burst."

"Damn you, Dominic," she moaned faintly, grabbing for the covers. "As Queen Victoria said, we are not amused. I'm tired and, as Garbo says, I want to be alone!"

"Darling, don't say that," he whispered, sitting down beside her. "You know what special talents I have. Between English nannies and Italian schools I knew more at sixteen than your American men know at forty. I'm right, you know. You confessed to me yourself that Max, poor bugger, might have kept you if he had my gifts."

"Leave Max out of this!" she raged. "I loved Max once and I've never loved you—ever. All you are to

66

me is a—stud! Jaded. Amoral. Wallowing in decay!" she spit at him. "Why don't you leave me alone, go out and find yourself a little boy or a rich old lady—or a goat!"

"You're being a shade unkind," he said, unruffled by her diatribe. "You know I prefer women and especially do I prefer you, Melissa, because you challenge me, you demand so much, you defy me to give you the impossible and I can still give you more than you bargained for."

He reached for the light switch.

"Leave it on," she ordered. "When I degrade myself I like to see what I'm doing. Don't delude *yourself*, Dominic. Don't think you mean enough for me to hate *myself* in the morning. I'm going to hate *you*!"

# SATURDAY

The magpie *maternae* attacked the dormant nest.

   Swooping.

   Picking.

   Snooping.

   Poking.

   Gaily plumaged (a perverse trait of the female of the species) she had the intrepid spirit of the scavenger, the keen eyesight of the *diurnal accipitridae*, or eagle, and beneath the fine feathers, a thick skin.

   She could pinpoint her prey however well camouflaged and pounce without mercy, or even a *merci*, confiscating the spoils with the righteous excuse that "it was for the best."

   Her primal need to take things and move them around often led to the disruption of other life cycles but true to the creed of the people-watchers, she chirped a melody stolen from the whippoorwill, "For the best . . . for the best . . . for the best . . ."

   Caught in the act of vandalism by a scandalized

victim, she might hesitate a moment only to continue her foray with no flutter of shame.

"MOTHER! What in God's name are you doing? Can't I leave you down here for five minutes?"

"Melissa, please don't raise your voice at your mother. I'm only doing a few of the things you apparently never think of doing or never have time for—though what you *do* do all day long with no job is a mystery to me! These books and that table are coated with dust and I can't stand being in the same room with them."

"Please, Mother. Give me that dustcloth. This is my house. I live here. I *like* dust."

"But it's filthy! You can't live in a pigsty! Finish whatever you were doing upstairs while I wash off these picture frames. I know I was early getting here. You know how I feel about punctuality. I always give myself an extra fifteen minutes to get places. I really ought to get into those closets of yours in the kitchen. Wash everything. Rearrange your dishes so you can *find* something—and some new paper lining, too. Something floral and gay. I can pick it up in the five-and-ten . . . That's the way to keep a home."

"That's the way to keep *your* home, not *my* home!" she retorted, controlling the urge to say more. It wouldn't help. It never had.

She took the offending rag from her mother's hands. "I know you know more about house-cleaning than any five maids, but please, it's the weekend, time to rest. Sit here . . . with your eyes closed if necessary. I'll get my bag and we can go."

She tried to think of some neutral remark to restore

69

mother-daughter rapport. "I'm starved!" Mothers always expected their young to be hungry. "Think of a fun place to go for lunch."

The house had become a relay station with arrivals and departures crazily avoiding collision by divine intervention. Bedroom farces were no fun if you were living the story line. Much earlier, Calvin had stumbled up to the bathroom and knocked on her door which somehow had been locked during the night. Calvin shouted his thanks for the hospitality. He was going home to face Quentin. Things looked brighter on a sunny morning.

Flattened against the shaded window, she had peered into the street, a counterspy in counterpane with a sheet wrapped round her, watching for Calvin's departure.

Her mother was due to arrive in half an hour for one of their many long-postponed lunch dates. With Calvin gone, Dominic lingered, unwilling to be dispatched posthaste. The impending maternal visit in no way dismayed Dominic nor hastened his morning ablutions.

"My dear girl. Surely your mother knows you have love affairs. I can't see why you're all nerves."

"Since I am a veteran of marriage," she said with annoyance, "she knows I am not exactly a virgin but I can't very well flaunt you before her, especially when you'll make no pretense about being in the neighborhood and just dropping in for a dish of tea."

"Ah—that would be sheer heaven. Be a good girl and brew me a cup while I bathe and shave. Your mother should be pleased that you have a considerate lover like me who doesn't desert you after getting what he wants, as you Americans so quaintly say, leaving you lonely and sobbing in the dark but instead holds you and cossets you like a cherished being until morning.''

"Dominic, please get out of here. Now!" Dominic hated leaving places. "She's coming at 11:30 . . ."

"What a barbaric hour for lunch!"

"We're going shopping first. If she sees you I'll never hear the end of it. We see each other very rarely and each time we argue and spit at each other. It's our chemistry, I guess. Today I'd like to have a nice peaceful time with her with as little grief as possible.''

"Maybe your mother will like me. How do you know? Why don't we wait and see?"

"Dominic . . . please . . . *please leave*! PLEASE, Dominic . . ."

Feverishly, she had made the bed, straightened the scattered books and magazines, dusted the window sills with a kleenex.

Dominic shrugged and dressed hurriedly. "There. Fully clothed for inspection. But don't look underneath. It's all decay. Now do I get me cup of tea?"

"No, Dominic. Please, darling. Go! I make lousy tea . . . with tea bags . . . please, please go. She's liable to come early and there's no back door.''

"In England coming early is considered more rude than coming late. I can always go back down over the balcony.''

Exasperation pushed her to the brink of tears. "No . . . no . . . no! If you stay one more minute, I'll never speak to you again!" Stamp foot. Turn back. Pout. Wait for next move.

"All right, darling. I'm off. We're dining tonight?

71

I'll check you later. Have a good day and speak kindly to your mum."

He had gone, without a word about taking her with him to the film studio in Brooklyn late in the afternoon as promised. It might be good experience for her to watch some film production, maybe help her career, change her entire life to be able to say, "Yes, of course, I do know a little something about film production."

Like so many others, it had been a loaded invitation, a promise of things to come in the future to enhance the purpose of things happening now. It fell into the category of "How would you like to sail to Bermuda? Some friends of mine have a sloop and they're going the first warm weekend" or "Next winter, I'm taking a lodge at Sun Valley and I want you to be my guest."

Future indefinite, they glorified the present indecisive. It disturbed Melissa that so many of the invitations that she had always regretted missing when chained to an office routine or marriage frequently dissolved into thin air now that she could accept them.

The last thing Melissa expected to be when she grew up was divorced.

Nothing in her upbringing prepared her for it. At high school there had been compulsory Personal Hygiene where the teacher faced them in an agony of terror and embarrassment, rolling and unrolling blurred charts and using medical terms which sent them scurrying to the unabridged dictionary with high hopes. On the subject of the vagina and penis, she had raced along in a garbled whisper, unable to shake her ingrained revulsion at saying the words aloud. On the subject of men-stru-a-tion, as the textbook specified pronunciation, she had traced its Latin root to pre-history and urged dry feet and extra sleep.

Kissing was discussed in terms of respiratory con-tagion and the spread of mononucleosis, said to be transferred orally. Other sexual functions were touched but lightly with her nervous pointer. To the girls' in-tense disappointment, whenever the fundamentals of reproduction seemed imminent, their expectant hush would scare her and back they would go to underarm deodorants, clean feet and regular bathing.

In Biology there had been pregnant frogs to take apart. Years later, having her first dinner in Paris with Don Kipcik, she had gagged at the sight of frog's legs, so persistent was her memory of the dead frog, pinned spread-eagle to the table, jellied embryo oozing from her middle.

Frogs did not get divorced. Only dissected.

At lunchtime, Melissa and her best friend, Dolores Easton, traded sandwiches and discussed their ambi-tions to be prostitutes. There had been stories in the papers about girls kidnapped off the streets and shipped to whore houses in Morocco. Walking home from school, they would linger in delicious suspense when-ever a suspicious car slowed down near them.

There was endless speculation as to what really hap-pened if you were a prostitute. What you said. How it felt to have intercourse with someone you weren't in *love* with. They worried about falling in love and wanting to give up the wicked life. Dolores said a medical student she knew told her it was *physically* impossible for men to tell whether you were a virgin or not so you could lie. Women were supposed to lie.

73

Men expected them to. Dolores had since become an actress specializing in tarnished women.

In an all-girl school, the chief topic of conversation, second only to boys, was breasts. How to make them bigger. How to make them smaller. Whether to make a boy stop above them or below them. Good friends would examine each other critically, advising the latest designs in bra magic or development cream.

A bombshell was dropped one day in the locker, room when one of the girls whispered excitedly, "Do you know what happens to your nipples when you have a baby?"

"Sure—they turn into a Milk Bar!" the class wit shrieked from the next aisle.

"No, no—they turn brown! They change from pink to brown!"

For months afterward, undressing for gym meant taking a quick look around to see if anyone had been an unwed mother.

At home, Melissa's mother had buck-passed the facts-of-life lecture to Ellis who kept saying, "you know what I mean?" She had finished by showing her little sister an illicit contraceptive with the parting advice, "If a boy makes a joke about wearing rubbers, make believe he thinks it's going to rain."

Before marrying Max, she had listened with amusement to Mother's garbled advice on what she kept calling The Nuptial Night. Claire deluded herself that Melissa at twenty-four had limited her social skirmishes to kissing games and her year in Europe to writing postcards.

The Nuptial Night was a cinch.

The Divorce Night was the rough one.

Zonite had not cottoned on to the ad possibilities. ''I cried the night I was divorced! Why didn't somebody tell me? . . .'' and all that.

If homosexuals were the Third Sex and neuters were the Unsex, what were divorcees? The Ex-Sex? The Hex-Sex? The Fourth Sex? Only if you were a newspaperman. Henry VIII didn't know what he started. Modern society hadn't yet made up its mind. In a system built on categories, here was a big chunk of population, ignored by the chart-makers and product-pushers.

Special needs were overlooked.

*The Divorce Cookbook: How To Eat Your Heart Out And Look Happy.*

*Redecorating for Divorce: How To Begin Again With Half Your Furniture.*

*The Alimony Guide: Separate Editions for Husbands and Wives.*

The trouble was everyone had always seemed so *happy* getting a divorce. Movie stars gaily announcing their careers kept them apart but they would always be friends, hubby mugging outrageously for the cameras to steal some of the attention from wifey's crossed thighs.

Las Vegas, Puerto Rico and the other separation centers were a houseparty for sun-tanned beauties in skimpy play clothes squired by handsome natives while waiting in ornate splendor for a ticket back to the open market.

Haggles over community property and the fantastic settlements made by multi-wed millionaires were to Melissa as unreal as England's royal family. She envied the ex-wives who got millions to ''live in the manner to which they had become accustomed'' especially when they were a car-hop or hat check girl before meeting the man with the gold-plated checkbook.

When her own turn came, it was like the abortion. Not too frightening in the abstract but more than she gargained for in actuality.

The divorce had left her high and dry on unfriendly soil. Neither fish nor fowl, she was fair game for the Dominics and Martins and Sams who hunted without ground rules. Once divorced, it was assumed your morality had slipped off with your wedding band. As it happened, Melissa's had preceded it.

She had loved Max and he had failed her. Now—would someone else like to try, someone out there in the shadows like to try and hit the mark? Don't be bashful! It's all good, clean fun! Gentlemen, step right up!

After college, she had played at fashion promotion as a Girl Friday at an agency and then spent that year in Europe and getting mixed up with Don Kipcik. Photographers were poison unless you took them a little at a time.

Now, at twenty-eight, her lack of professional training and experience was matched only by a profound disinterest in starting at the bottom. She didn't want to be a career girl that badly.

Yet her conscience reminded her she was the party pooper, the one who said she was tired and didn't want to play. She felt guilty about taking money from a man with whom she wouldn't live. The alternatives were no brighter.

Move in with mother?

It would be more restful in the subway.

Share an apartment?

She had lived in the Village with three girls that first year out of college. Once married you could not return to the sorority.

Money was why she hated to see Max. His face reminded her she was getting not giving. She had taken her Divorce Vows: "I, Melissa, take thee, Max, for all I can get . . ."

He had given her the one thing she wanted, and then taken it away. Poor little rich wife. On the bum. Living on a handout. Looking for an answer. On the bum. Looking for a man. On the bum.

She often reminded herself that Max had a good income and the divorce was his fault anyway. He owed her something. Still, she preferred having the checks deposited directly into her bank account. It heightened the illusion of found money from an unknown benefactor.

It was ironic that you got paid more for being a bad wife than a good wife. A good wife couldn't go to court and say her husband was being stingy whereas an ex-wife could tie up his salary or threaten him with jail if he didn't come across. No wonder some men hated women.

Overheard at any cocktail party:

"And what do you do for a living?"

"Oh, I collect alimony. Very hard work opening up those envelopes."

Thousands of women with wedding rings tucked away as souvenirs or sold for old gold, hesitating to marry again because the alimony stops. Wallowing in

77

the morass called getting back into circulation. Circles, the art of going around in.

Melissa always came back to one idea which she could not escape. If you took money from a man you were a whore. What was lower than a whore? If you took money from a man for doing absolutely nothing, you were lower than a whore. You were a divorcee.

Her only salvation was to start feeling useful again. To make money in business you had to spend money. To swim in the mainstream of life, she would have to leave the side streets, the quiet times of day, the stealthiness of night and rejoin the earth people. She might be swamped in the current at first or bruised on the rocks but it might be worth it. It would have to be.

She would have to accen-tu-ate the positive from now on, eliminate the frantic screams of ''No—no-no-no . . .'' Become a Yes-Woman. A yes-woman who knew how to say No and make them like it. She would show the Mothers of the World that she could succeed without having children as an excuse for failure as a woman. She would turn invertebrate. Impregnate herself with a new life. Discard the old.

Some day, she would add up how much Max had given her and return it all in crisp new bills tied up in a red ribbon. Reimbursement in full for services not rendered.

She had meant to get up early and clean before her mother's arrival. God knows she wanted to be friends with her mother but it never worked out that way. Something always blew up in their faces.

Living in the heart of New York with coal particles,

industrial smoke and the choking debris of new buildings under construction made it impossible to keep a spotless home. Even with the windows closed, grit filtered through the cracks and coated everything.

A little dust didn't bother Melissa. In matters of housekeeping, she lived by the Dusty Rule, the concept of Clean Slobbery, the theory that books and magazines left carelessly about collected no more grime than those militantly quartered on shelves.

She was a firm believer in personal cleanliness, skin, nails and hair. She imposed on herself strict rules about combs, hairbrushes, powder puffs, wash cloths, underwear and white gloves, all of which she kept immaculate.

On the other hand, shoes romped beneath her bed in merry disunion, skirts bedecked the chairs in that state of suspended animation achieved by throwing, and sweaters and coats defied recognition by always having one sleeve pulled inside out from the impatience of removal.

Newspapers accumulated for days until she threw them all out including the articles she wanted to read. Black-bottomed coffee cups collected on dressing table, bathtub ledge, bedside and book shelves until the weekly maid washed them all at once.

Melissa's attitude toward homemaking had solidified after reading an article in a woman's magazine which stated that meticulous housekeepers were sexually frustrated. They took it out on themselves and their men by emptying ashtrays between puffs, vacuuming under foot and declaring certain areas out-of-bounds such as the front door and bedspreads. Restrictive inhibition of the natural tendencies, like toilet training. Dirt, like sex, was a constant temptation to the weakness of man, a constant reproach to the vulnerability of woman.

"This couch looks like somebody slept on it," her mother grumbled, punching up the pillows.

"Somebody did!" Melissa said defiantly.

"What! Do you mean—"

"It was a joke, mother. Come on. I'm ready. The stores will be crowded today. It's Saturday. Let's go to Lord & Taylor. We can shop first and eat in the soup bar."

She had lost her appetite.

"Soup bar? You can't carry on a conversation on a counter stool."

That was the idea. Lots of talk but no conversation.

"Melissa, I hate to tell you this—"

*Oop! Here we go.*

"What, mother?"

"Your sleeves are too long. They should be a good half-inch shorter."

"I like them this way, Ma. I have cold wrists."

*Please, no more.*

"If you'll get me some pins, I'll pin them up for you. Then you can hem them. Take you a minute. You're a very handy girl with a needle when you want to be."

"Mother!" Quietly now. Firmly now. "Mother. I like this suit. I like the color. I like the style and I like the sleeves. Just the way they are. Can we please go?"

Claire Murdock *tchicked* her tongue behind her teeth. Melissa was a lost cause. What was the younger generation coming to and all that. If only her father were alive! Still, during their eighteen-year-marriage,

Arthur Murdock had tried to be a father to Melissa, at least at the beginning, despite the child's resentment of the marriage so soon after Will Verdon's death.

She remembered the clammy afternoon in their Riverside Drive apartment when Melissa returned from school and called her a magpie.

Belligerently, the child had read from her notebook, "The magpie, in common with the raven, the jay and many birds of prey, has a remarkable capacity, when its mate dies, for obtaining a new mate within a day or two."

Claire's most-repeated remark was that she did not understand her daughter. She believed in a mother's duty, however, and would never be found lacking there. She had a responsibility and meant to see it through.

"I'm ready, dear," she said, pummeling a last pillow on their way out.

Thank God they were on their way. Melissa kicked herself for not meeting Claire at the shop. Her coming here never failed to cause an imbroglio, even before the divorce nightmare. She simply could not keep her grubby hands off Melissa's things.

—Is *this* how you keep a linen closet?

—To look in that refrigerator, all you eat is martinis.

—Why don't you move the couch around *this* way?

—*Nobody's* bedroom looks like this.

— . . . that lamp . . .

— . . . those tables . . .

"Shall we take a bus or a cab?" Melissa opened the door.

"I've been meaning to discuss one other thing with

81

"You've mentioned it twice. Once right now."

"Well . . . did you check into your insurance like I asked you to? Make sure you're covered? If any delivery boy or the postman or anyone trips on this, you can be sued for damages! Go into hock for life!"

It was the new owner's responsibility but Melissa hadn't told her mother about the changeover and her impending eviction. Claire's response to trouble was of such emotional intensity that she diverted anxiety from the cause to herself.

"Okay, Mother. I'll look into it. Whatever you say."

Yes her to death.

She signalled a taxi, determined to outfumble on the fare.

Glimpsing their reflection as they paused to look at the window display, Melissa felt a surge of pride at being part of a chic mother-and-daughter ensemble, the slightly taller, younger image of the slim, stylish woman at her side, a combination worthy of presiding over a charity tea.

Inside Lord & Taylor, an astute saleswoman asked if they were sisters which cheered Claire and forced an inane smile on Melissa's face. She didn't want to be sisters with her mother.

For lunch, they found a small Italian restaurant on Madison Avenue at 38th Street, the lower edge of Advertising Row where the prices had not yet caught up with expense account potential.

Even before the antipasto, Claire began the Inquisition.

you, Missy. It's this grate. It's very dangerous. I've mentioned it to you a dozen times.''

"Has Max been sending your checks all right?"

"Yes, mother. He's very reliable. The money is deposited in my account every Friday. Like clockwork."

"You mean he doesn't send it to you at home? Be sure you check to see that he sends the right amount."

"Oh, Mother, can't you stop? Can't you ever stop? Max has been generous and kind. He is giving me a substantial chunk of his earnings which is extremely generous when you consider that I divorced *him*. He has been solicitous and helpful and never once have I had to call him and ask for the money."

"I'm only thinking of you and your happiness, Melissa. If he's so reliable and wonderful, why did you divorce him in the first place?"

There were certain intimate facts that embarrassed mothers.

"Let's drop it, Mom. You never really listen anyway. All you do is talk."

"All right—we can discuss something else. Have you found a job yet?"

Another revolving door.

"As you know—if you ever listened that is—I'm not looking for a job. I'm free-lancing."

"You mean sleeping til noon every day."

"I am trying, very desperately because my very existence depends on it, to find a way to express myself. I have creative instincts, Mother, and I want to use them. I find great peace and security in ceramics, in working with fabrics and designs. If I had gone to an art school instead of that fancy secretarial school you insisted would do me so much good after college, I'd be five years ahead of myself."

"I was only thinking of your income. You can't hold your head up these days without money. Nobody cares how creative you are, you still have to be able to pay your way. Your trouble is you think you're too good for everything. For me, your father—"

"—he's *not* my father—"

"—for Max—for working eight hours a day like every other girl."

"I'm *not* every other girl. I'm not a carbon copy and I want to try to find my own way!"

"Well . . . I was only trying to make a little conversation, that's all."

They ate in silence, Melissa searching her mind for safe topics. Recipes. TV. Movies.

"It shouldn't cost too much," Claire ruminated.

"What shouldn't, mother?" New drapes?

"That grate . . ."

"Oh, for God's sake!" She threw her fork down, splashing oil and vinegar on the table. "Mother, why is it completely impossible for you to treat me like an ordinary human being? Like one of your friends, for instance. Why does my being your daughter prevent you from giving me the common, everyday courtesy you'd give a perfect stranger?"

"But you're not a stranger, or a friend. You're my own flesh and blood."

"And you can't respect that. Maybe you don't respect yourself and that's why you don't respect me!"

"Missy! How can you say that to me—your mother!"

"That's just it. How can you say the things you say to me—your daughter? And do the things you do? Would you walk into anyone else's home and start dusting and re-arranging things and cleaning out closets and telling the person who lived there it was a pigsty? Or suddenly become high priestess of fashion and criticize her clothes without being asked?''

''But I'm your mother and mothers have rights where their children are concerned!''

''If mothers treated their children with the respect and courtesy they reserve for other people there wouldn't be so much friction. Questions! Questions! Questions! Why don't you do this? Why don't you do that? Warning me to check up on Max as if he were a sneak, trying to chisel me out of my alimony when I'm not looking. Max has been very decent and I won't have you maligning him.''

''You certainly have a peculiar attitude, defending him against me! I'll never understand these civilized divorces.'' A nervous finger twisted her pearls. ''I can't think why in the world you divorced him. No wife was ever more loyal.''

''Oh, Mother, you insist on being bull-headed. A man doesn't become an ogre because a marriage falls apart.''

''I warned you not to marry him.''

Old hash. Warmed over. Slightly sick-making.

''You warned me not to marry *anyone*. You liked having me home so you could read my mail and poke through my dresser when I was out.''

(The cruel shaft.)

''How can you say such a thing?''

''Because it's true and I caught you at it.''

''I wanted you to be happy.'' Repeat refrain, same old verse, only worse. ''You've always accused me of not taking an interest in you. When I *do* take an

85

interest you say I'm interfering, spying on you. I've always tried to be a good mother to you, especially after your poor father died.''

"Oh, yes!" The wound still festered. Her eyes blazed. Her mouth curled in contempt. "For a whole six weeks you mourned him and then it was all to much for you. You couldn't stand sleeping alone in daddy's big bed. You had to take the insurance money and go out and buy a new stud!''

Claire slapped her face so quickly that no one saw it, including Melissa. "You're a twisted, spiteful girl!" She left in the middle of the scallopine.'

*Damn her, damn her, damn her!* Damn my father for leaving me. And damn her for stiffing me with the lousy lunch check.

She finished lunch and called in to her service from the phone booth in the ladies room. Only Ingrid had checked in to ask if she wanted to go shopping this afternoon.

A little more shopping might be soothing. She caught Ingrid on her way out and returned to the table for another cup of coffee before meeting at Saks. She buried her mother under an avalanche of speculation on what happened between Philip and Ingrid the night before.

"Bernard's giving me a prezzie and I want you to help me pick it out," Ingrid greeted her, serene and slender in sea-green wool. When particularly smug, Ingrid resorted to baby-talk, for which Melissa could cheerfully wallop her.

"But when did this happen? Did you late-date him after Philip went home?''

She smiled enigmatically.

"No—better than that. I wasn't home when he called last night. He was absolutely wild on the phone this morning, blasted me out of a deep sleep at nine o'clock, couldn't wait any later. Said he tried me for hours last night, every twenty minutes until he fell asleep with the light on. So I pointed out to him that he had no right to check up on me and then he apologized and asked where I wanted to have dinner tonight and I just pouted—the wronged angel—and he said what was I doing this afternoon and I said I was going shopping and made it sound far more exciting than any possible expedition with *him* and by this time he was really miserable but trying to be gay and said let's pretend today's a holiday and because it's a holiday I have to give you a present so when you're shopping this afternoon choose anything you like and charge it to me and wear it tonight as a surprise!"

"Ingrid—" Melissa couldn't help being impressed. "You're amazing! The Princess in the Ivory Tower, deigning to grant Bernard the supreme pleasure of buying you the most exquisite dress in New York."

"If it gives him pleasure, what else is important? I'm sure his mother would agree," Ingrid said with mock piety. "And he didn't specify dress. He said anything I wanted. Do you think a chinchilla coat would be carrying things too far?"

"No, no . . . it's a great idea. I can borrow it."

"I have half a mind to do it," she nibbled her lip in excitement. "But no—I'm playing for higher stakes. I can wait for the chinchilla until after we're married. If I got it now, his mother would be sure to hear about it and tell him what a gold-digger I am."

"How dare she!" Melissa giggled.

"How dare she indeed! Let's go find me some simple little $500 Givenchy."

"But tell me, what happened with Philip? I'm gasping to know. I half-expected you to turn up with a jar of Pond's in one hand and a soupy smile."

"No, I'm sorry to disappoint you. The kind of engagement he had in mind was too sophisticated for apple blossoms."

"Same old jazz?"

"Same old jazz," she sighed. "My only satisfaction is knowing that he wanted me very badly last night. It was all I could do to stay slightly out of reach—inviting yet remote—as tantalizing as I could be without being cheap, when all I wanted to do was get out of that dress and into his arms. The zipper was on his side, too. Pinched like hell. I'm getting fat."

"I've heard abstinence makes the heart grow fonder."

"According to Mother Goose maybe. All he did was take his punishment like a little gentleman. He's clever. He wouldn't allow his passions to get out of hand. He'd have been married long before this."

"Well, anyway . . . you made Bernard nervous."

"Yes . . . and he'll be more nervous when he sees the bill I'm going to run up this afternoon. I think you should have something new, too, M'liss. Let's let Bernard Nahoum buy us both something."

Eight hundred and thirty-four dollars later they were in Melissa's living room, shoes off, exulting over their purchases when the doorbell rang.

"Mrs. Max Kempton?"

"Yes."

"Madam, you are served. Sorry, lady." He thrust an envelope into her hand and walked quickly away.

"Oh, no . . . No . . !"

"My God in Heaven . . . who died?" Ingrid rushed to her friend's side, crossing herself from long-forgotten habit.

"Nobody died—unless you count me! I've been evicted. Here's the notice. They finally got me. I have to be out by Thursday. Five days! Or the sheriff or somebody will come and toss me out on the sidewalk."

"Oh, Missy . . . isn't there something we can do—call a lawyer—get an appeal—something?"

"No. I've been through the mill. I guess you could say they've got me where I live!" She began to laugh and cry. "What am I going to do? Where am I going to go? The YWCA?"

"Calm yourself. Let's talk the thing out. If necessary you can move in with me for a while. We'll think of something."

The phone.

"Bells! Bells! Bells! I feel like Edgar Allen Poe. All they bring is trouble."

Walter Simpson had picked the wrong time to call.

"You ghoul!" she shrieked. "Couldn't wait one minute to gloat over my corpse! Couldn't wait to find out how I would take it!"

"What are you talking about? What's happening?"

"Don't pretend you don't know. An extremely polite man has just handed me an eviction notice. Outsville! The plantation has been sold. It's white slavery or starve for little old Magnolia. What I should do is commit suicide and leave a note saying I was persecuted into it. Put a curse on the house! Who would

89

move in then? You'd have a haunted house on your hands and good riddance!''

"Melissa . . . M'liss . . . now take it easy. Now stop crying . . . Now please take it easy. It can't be that bad.''

"But it is! It is! Can't you understand? I have to be out of here by *Thursday*! My furniture. My clothes. Everything! And where am I supposed to go? The Florence Crittenden Home? Maybe I can get pregnant by Thursday and they'll take me in.''

"Melissa . . .'' he said quietly.

Only sobs.

"Melissa . . . please answer me.''

"Yes . . .''

"Melissa . . . I'm very sorry about this. You know I've had nothing to do with it. The reason I called was to ask you to dinner tonight, if you were free, that is, so we could talk some more about the house.''

At least the convicted girl would eat well.

"I'm only suggesting we do it this way because I figured you'd be meeting up with your pals at Morocco later in the evening,'' he went on with just a hint of malice. "So I thought we could have dinner and then I'd drop you wherever you have to be.''

"In plenty of time for your late date.''

Sly.

". . . Yes . . . you might say that . . .''

Defensive.

"The redhead?''

"My, but you have total recall. What color eyes do I have?''

She bit her tongue. Her mind had swept a 180 degree arc that curved like this: Ditch Dominic for dinner.

90

Prevail on Walter to somehow rescind the eviction and live happily ever after. No. Refuse Walt's invitation. His late date smacked of an insult. No. Accept Walt's invitation. Meet Dominic afterwards. Have cake and eat it, too. Try avoid indigestion.

"You've fit into my evening perfectly, Walter," she said smoothly. "I'm due at Morocco at eleven."

Maybe she would post an "Apartment Wanted" notice in the ladies room.

Ingrid stood straight and tall, exuding strength and comfort. "Everything will be all right. We'll think of something." She believed in repetition as a precursor to truth.

Deadly calm now, Melissa called Dominic. She could not meet him until eleven. Take it or leave it. He took it. He was just leaving for the studio in Brooklyn. Did she want to come along?

NO!

"Why don't you call Max, too?" Ingrid suggested. "Maybe with his airlines connections he can help you. Surely he'll do something."

"Sure . . . increase my alimony maybe? All he can think of in time of trouble is to fork over a few bucks! Still, there are things here that belong to him, that he said he wanted if I ever decided to move or—or remarry. He was very sweet really, didn't want to take anything away because he thought 'our home' should stay intact."

"If he's as considerate as all that, he won't let you go through this mess all by yourself without lifting a finger to help you. Call him. Maybe it's not too late."

"Oh, Ingrid . . ." she sighed. "You do believe in magic wands and fairy tale princesses don't you? Find

91

the prince with the heart of gold, repeat the secret words and abracadabra, all the evil spirits vanish.''

"I just think women shouldn't have to handle big problems. Men are supposed to do it for them.''

"We know that, but do they?''

Max lived in one of those de-personalized apartment hotels inhabited by the homeless of above average income plus a wealthy recluse or two of Hetty Green eccentricity.

Mr. Kempton was not in.

So far as the operator knew he had not gone away for the weekend.

She would be happy to give him the message.

What made operators so happy?

"This is Mrs. Kempton calling.'' He might think it was his mother. "*Melissa* Kempton, that is. Please tell Mr. Kempton that I would like him to come for drinks tomorrow about four-ish. Very important.''

Ingrid grinned. "Sounds like a British spy story. I'm going to stir up some martinis. I think you can use a drink.''

"Good idea. At the rate the two of us are going, we'll wind up with the bottle and each other.''

"I like you but not that much. If you're going into battle with Mr. Simpson and his T-square tonight you'd better do something about your hair. From the back it looks like birds' nest soup without the soup. Who flattened it out for you last night, as if I didn't know?''

"Nothing like that,'' she lied for no particular reason. "I was just restless. Calvin brought his troubles over. Quentin is being ditsy about losing his doormat.''

"Well, let's adjourn to your dressing room while I pin up the back of your head. I've been itching to try on some of your jewelry, too."

"It's all junk except for my rings."

"Doesn't matter. Nobody wears real jewelry. Keep it in the vault. Everyone just *assumes* you have the real McCoy stashed away with your securities."

Ingrid studied her $100-an-hour face in the three-way mirror, every flaw cruelly magnified by the harsh bright light Melissa insisted was necessary for personal grooming. You fooled nobody but yourself putting on makeup in a soft, flattering light and then stepping out into merciless sunshine.

"Is there anyone else who can help?" Ingrid asked. "With all the people you know, somebody should do something."

" 'Fraid not," Melissa said, filing her nails. "We're all much too sophisticated to help each other, perish forbid. It's bad taste even to ask. To enjoy this life you have to be healthy, wealthy and fast on your feet. Our trouble is we're vulnerable, like Marguerite Gautier—a little hard luck or a bad cough and everyone runs for the hills."

"Camille? She was a jerk. She played the courtesan too long. That's a mistake I'm not going to make. I'm going to get married and with all the pomp and ceremony of the most fashionable society wedding of the year. No beer hall in the Bronx for me. I don't care whether it's Temple Emanu-El or St. Thomas's. I've had my nose pressed against the windowpane too long. I want in and it doesn't matter to me whether I turn Protestant or Jewish so long as I get carried over the threshold."

93

"But you'd rather have Philip than Bernard."

"Frankly, yes. Nobody wants to be Jewish unless they can't help themselves."

"Okay. Cross off one Jew. But let's keep the presents. I like my new cashmere shawl even if he doesn't know he's given it to me."

"Well, then, that leaves Philip." She threw back her head in a wild, bitter laugh. "Isn't this the absolute end? Here we're trying to decide which one I should marry and neither one of them has proposed."

They clinked glasses, drained them and refilled them from the icy pitcher nested among the hairpins, jars, cotton, spray cans and scented boxes.

"We shouldn't drink anymore," Melissa said. "Bad for our aging skin." She leaned closer to the mirror. "See those adorable laugh lines around the eyes? In another year they'll be crying."

Ingrid flapped her fingers under her chin in firming motion. "Jowls! Another year and I'll be wearing a veil draped around my throat to hide the droop."

"I found a gray hair the other day."

"Where?"

"Right in the middle."

Ingrid stopped her pincurl operation to find the hair. "Got it. Hand me your eyebrow tweezer and I'll yank it right out."

"No. You can't. I'll get twenty more in its place."

"Baloney. Give it to me."

"Finish your drink. Alcohol is a good preservative. It will keep you young."

"Splendid idea . . . we're getting old . . . might as well enjoy it. When I get married I'll be known as the 'mature' bride . . . a vision in lavendar and an old lace wedding gown.''

"And I'll make a *trompe l'oeil* out of my eviction notice as a wedding gift. Pour some ketchup on it to look like blood—*my* blood!''

"The hell with it!'' Ingrid swayed where she sat, spraying clouds of setting lotion on the network of pincurls spread over her friend's head. "Let's forget about men! Let's give 'em the shiv, as we used to say in my old neighborhood. We can go into the fashion business. Open our own boutique. Join forces with Calvin. Cater to all our social friends. Make a mint . . . a chocolate-covered after-dinner mint!''

"I've got an even better idea. Why don't you get your close personal buddy Bernard to buy back this little house and we could open shop here—'The Carriage House for the Carriage Trade'—and we can pay him off slowly . . .''

"*Ve-e-e-ry* slowly . . .''

"We'll charge outrageous prices and make them fight for the privilege of paying!''

"Good taste comes high!''

"Wait . . . wait . . . I've got another brilliant idea, Ingrid! We have to be ultra-exclusive, don't we? Exclusive means you have to exclude somebody so let's keep out mothers! No mothers allowed!''

"Inspired! Perfectly inspired! No mothers! Mothers Go Home! Mothers Drop Dead! Let's knock off a few mothers right now.''

Flushed from the gin and her own excitement, Ingrid pulled a silk scarf from around her neck and thrust some cotton into the center. Working dextrously with a few rubber bands she formed a primitive rag doll.

"Voodoo . . ." she whispered, giggling. "Who do? We do! Let's voodoo mother! Get some pins."

"Hey . . . me, too. I have a score to settle with a certain M-O-T-H-E-R. . . ." She found a stray tennis sock in the bottom drawer, and feverishly stuffed the remaining cotton into it. "Double, double, toil and trouble . . ."

"That's no good. Shakespeare didn't do spook stuff."

"Yeah, what about that kook, King Lear? And what about . . ."

"It wasn't voodoo."

"Well, what do we chant then? Here are some hat pins."

"I don't know. They do voodoo in Louisiana and in Haiti—places like that where they speak French. Maybe we should say something in French. Whose mother are you doing? I'm doing Bernard's. She'll leave all her jewelry to Bernard and he'll give it to me. You doing your own or Max's?"

Melissa hesitated. However tainted, blood was thicker than water, and she had hurt her mother enough for one day. "Max's mother! The *other* Mrs. Kempton. She killed something for me and I'll never forgive her. Never! Never! Never!" She began sticking the hat pin into the bulging sock.

"That's a good word! Never! *Jamais! Jamais!* Never! Never! *Jamais!* Never Never! Never!" Intoxicated with equal parts martini and hysteria, they sat side by side, gleefully plunging the hat pins into the figures, swaying back and forth, changing the word "Never" and stamping their feet in rhythm.

96

"I've got a new one," Ingrid panted. "Die! *Meurs*! *Meurs*!"

"*Meurs*! *Meurs*!" Melissa echoed, her fingers tight about the doll's neck. The momentum of her thrust plunged the hat pin deep into the fleshy part of her thumb. Blood gushed over the white sock as she screamed, "My God! My God! I've really killed her! *Meurs*! *Meurs*! *Meurs*!" She thrust the bloody pin again and again into the sock, then hurled it into the basket under the dressing table.

"Cut it out," Ingrid said, suddenly sober. "We were only playing around."

Melissa was shaken. "There was blood all over her. I killed her. I got blood all over her. My blood!"

Ingrid fished it out of the basket. "Missy . . . look . . . it's an old tennis sock. And the two of us were so stoned from martinis you couldn't even see your own hand."

Melissa smiled weakly. "I sure get carried away. The Russians could brain wash me in sixty seconds flat." Gingerly, she dismantled the doll, threw away the sock and replaced the cotton in its container. It was clean. The blood had not seeped through to soil it.

"Got her right in the head," Melissa attempted to recapture their earlier mood. "The least I can hope for is that she has a splitting headache."

Ingrid's voodoo mother was back around her neck as a scarf. She moistened her gin-dry lips with her tongue. "It's homesville for me. Got to get tarted up in my new dress. Let's have a sobering cup of coffee and I'm off. Tonight I'm going to be a gold bobbie pin."

97

"What's a gold bobbie pin?"

"Well, Melissa, you're what I'd call a quasi gold bobbie pin. You don't belong to any minority group. You're good-looking. You went to an acceptable college and you have style. But the real gold bobbie pin is the unattainable ethnic dream girl of nice Jewish boys like Bernard. She's an alumna of Smith or Vassar or Wellesley or any number of finishing schools. She wears pleated skirts, cashmere sweaters with white Peter Pan collars and a tiny row of pearls. Her features are small, her hair usually blonde and straight and in it she wears a gold bobbie pin. She scares hell out of men who are not her masculine counterpart yet they want her, especially the nice Jewish boys, because she represents a complete break from any taint of immigrant life or the social and financial hazards of being one of the minority."

Melissa knew the type all too well and what offended her most was a certain sexless quality that had made her feel guilty about necking on a double date. "They're the first ones with their pants off if they wear them at all."

"I know," Ingrid said. "But they do it out of disdain—not kicks or love or excitement or any healthy reasons. When I first got to Paris, I met lots of them, studying at the Sorbonne. The French boys told them they were too flat-chested. But I must confess they were what I wanted to be when I was growing up. I always envied the girls in the college issues of the magazines and was I surprised when I got into the modelling business. Some of those *girls* are 30-year-old mothers and most of them never finished high school."

"One American myth shot to hell. So tonight is gold bobbie pin night?"

"Yes—I'm going to close in on him from two directions. A daring dress that seethes with continental enchantment and straight blonde hair held in place with a gold bobbie pin."

Walter could think of no valid reason for taking Melissa to dinner other than a selfless desire to change her life. Being so well-adjusted himself, he pictured Walter Simpson as Jesus Christ in a Brooks Brothers suit, ministering to the fallen, bolstering the weak, helping the sad-eyed girls to face another day.

Melissa was obviously in trouble. She needed him. In a different way from the redhead who couldn't pay for her dancing lessons or the big brunette who was afraid of becoming a lesbian or the throbbing mass of girls who drank too much, smoked too much and slept around too much, too often, too easily.

While he could not exactly point to any conspicuous successes among his personal projects, he nonetheless prided himself on contributing to the betterment of humanity by succoring these flotsam and jetsam treading water in a dark, dark sea.

Because it is said to have an unsettling effect on the gonads, Melissa wore red, Grecian-inspired in flowing chiffon with gold twine criss-crossing her ribs and cupping each breast separately. Floating chiffon panels cascaded from one shoulder. Closing her eyes, she aimed the perfume atomizer and sprayed her entire body from head to toe including the bends in her arms and the hem of the dress.

Downstairs she set the stage with candle light and

an LP of cool jazz sobbing out the blues in the far corner of the room. A dusty can of liver paste had been transformed into paté with a sprinkling of hard-boiled egg set in a circle of onion flavored crackers.

"You're hardly a creature of sorrow tonight, looking like this," he said with admiration.

"What did you expect? Sack cloth and ashes? I appreciate your concern, but please don't expect to find me bent over a suicide note. Now, what would you like to know about the house? You're the enemy so I'll only tell you the bad things."

"You lead. I'll follow."

In the basement, she pointed out the sweat-damp walls, rusty pipes and rat holes. He noted the neat kiln, considerable head room and the fact that they were not rat holes.

Upstairs, she showed him the leaky kitchen sink, sagging floor boards in the hallway and uninhabitable backyard. He saw the high ceilings, roomy kitchen and the possibility of converting the yard into a solarium with a glass roof.

Finally, she bemoaned the bathroom fixtures, the sparsity of closets and a leak in the roof which she assured him flooded her bedroom during storms. He approved the bathroom tiles, mentally measured spaces for built-in closets and stepped over the window ledge for a look at the street from the tiny balcony. (Men could not resist balconies.)

"Well?" she asked when they were settled again in the living room.

"Well?" he answered, nursing his drink. "I will say in my report that the most valuable asset of the house is its current tenant."

"Then why not let me stay?" She leapt to the advantage.

"It's not up to me and you know it."

"Well, then . . ."

"Well, then . . ."

"What do you think of the house structurally and so on? The possibilities in terms of your client."

"To be perfectly candid, the whole house is coming down on your head, bit by bit. I would recommend stripping it down to its skeleton, and if that's as strong as I think it, work from there."

"But the street footage is only fifteen feet. You can't build higher than three stories on frontage that small. What's the point of building? How can you make a profit on your investment?"

"I see you've been reading up on your real estate. You're right. We can't go higher than three stories on fifteen feet."

What he neglected to mention was that they had purchased the two adjoining brownstones as well and while it would take months of negotiations to get all the people out and begin demolition, his company had embarked on a policy of first-things-first, with Melissa topping the list because her ouster would mark the file on the little carriage house "Complete." Everything came down to bookkeeping in the end, regardless of esthetics.

"Why, yes," she said breathlessly. "I've done some extensive reading and research on the real estate laws. Fascinating restrictions—to protect the tenant, of course."

"Of course." He knew she was bluffing but it amused him.

"So—" she continued, tucking her legs under her on the couch beside him. "So—since you can't go any higher than three floors and since it's obviously poor economics to put so much money into re-doing a house that can only bring in a few paltry rents, why don't you say it isn't worth the effort and recommend they drop the whole idea?"

She hugged her knees. The ingenuous touch.

He felt like uncle teasing teen-age niece.

"What about the small matter of their investment in buying the property? Should they forget about that, mark it off as a foolish little tax loss?"

"No—" She hadn't thought of that. "Well . . . tell them to put it back on the market, resell it, maybe make an enormous profit!"

"Unless the new owner is you, they're going to want you out anyway."

"Yes, but it will take weeks and weeks of negotiating the sale and then the new owner will have to start from scratch to evict me and that will take months!"

He chuckled. "The mind of a woman at work. How can we win?" He took her hand. "Who wants to win?"

"Have some home-made imported paté."

"You bake it in that oven downstairs?"

"No, I force-fed a goose who happened by and took its liver. Very messy."

"Tastes like liver paste to me."

"There you go, destroying the illusion. Destroy. Destroy. Destroy. How could you tell it's liver paste?"

"You forget. I'm living the life of a bachelor and I pride myself on how fast I can open a can of liver

102

paste. A girl I used to know, that is I still know her but don't—ah . . .''

"See her anymore?"

"Yes. Well, she's a copywriter on one of those liver pastes and taught me all kinds of erotic things like mixing it into scrambled eggs, spicing it up with pickle relish and God knows what else. She sent me a case of the stuff.''

"And then?"

(Get him to talk about himself. Men liked that.)

"And then I wouldn't marry her so she gave me the fast shuffle. She knew exactly what I had in mind from the very beginning. I was married—though single—with no intention of getting a divorce. She seemed to think she could change my mind, that I was the boy to save her from—well, she finally saw I meant what I said about marriage. The last I heard she married a South American and is taking bull-fighting lessons on the Pampas.''

"What did she want you to save her from?"

"Well . . .'' he squirmed uncomfortably. "It's kind of personal.''

She persisted. "She's in South America. I don't even know her name. Please tell me. I'm dying to know.''

"Well . . . curiosity turned the cat's face red.'' He lit a cigarette and squinted at her through the smoke. "Expressed as delicately as possible, the young lady found it impossible to achieve—ah, sexual fulfillment—despite an extensive—ah, track record, you might say . . .''

"Until she met you?"

He shrugged deprecatingly. "Well, yes . . . but as

I explained to her, physiologically and psychologically she was just about ready to respond and I happened to be in the—ah, driver's seat at the time. This is getting worse and worse. Let's go find some dinner.''

"No—no—I'm fascinated. What a career you could have! I could set you up for a lecture tour of five hundred fraternity houses just like that. We'd clean up. 'How To Make Them Wake Up Screaming' by Walter Simpson.''

He was not amused.

"Come on, baby. Dinner. Let's go.''

"No!'' she pouted. "Not until we settle my housing problem. Will you or will you not tell Kelly and Karr they goofed, the house is built on marshland, you'll have to import dredging equipment from the Cameroons and the house isn't worth tearing down?''

The joke had gone too far. He stood and walked to the fireplace, leaning an elbow on the mantel. "I like you, Melissa, and I like your little house. Charming the way you've fixed it up—and only $90 rent in mid-Manhattan—and on the east side, too. It's a pity to move you out.''

"Then I can stay? Oh, Walter . . .''

The shimmering red chiffon alternately burned and cooled him like the sun on a windy day.

"Hold on now . . . Let's examine this clinically. I'd be risking a lot, my professional integrity in fact, sticking my neck out for you. What's in it for me?''

(Jocularity wins the day, he thought.)

But he was wrong. The joke had indeed gone too far. Gimmee Girl with cheek of brass was considering her next move. Before stopping to think how it might sound, she sank back in the couch, her arms behind her head and whispered, "Me . . ." Madame Recamier incarnate.

Taken aback and wishing he had never started the foolish little game she took so seriously, he laughed with rude intent. How could she be so thick? "What makes you think your precious body is worth taking all that trouble? Let me tell you, a love affair with a building is a million times more rewarding than a woman. At least when it's over, there's something solid you can look back on—something you can be proud of."

She felt suddenly cheap and ridiculous in the red dress and the seductive pose, as if he had tricked her into wearing a costume when there was no masquerade.

"Don't ennoble yourself, Walter. You're nothing but a face-lifter, a cosmetologist, and like everybody else, you have to do what the customer wants, including gargoyles spouting ginger ale if necessary! Don't give me the poetry of plastics. You belong at Helena Rubenstein's, shovelling mud on some great stone face, putting bright new facades on old wrecks, salvaging the foundations but . . ."

"Shut up! You talk too much. If only women could remember not to talk so Goddam much! You know who you remind me of? I'm old enough to be your father but you remind me of my mother! Crazy, isn't it?"

(With one word he had destroyed her composure.)

"—and do you know why you remind me of Mom? Because your idea of getting what you want is to wheedle for it, unfairly, outrageously, and all on a personal but-it's-only-little-me basis. I'd love to watch you try to get a loan from a bank. What do you do? Offer yourself as collateral? Or a nice home-cooked meal? You women want to compete in the grown-up world but you don't want to play by the rules. You complain about unfair treatment but you don't know the meaning of straightforward bargaining. You have to be devious, slinking through dark alleys, jumping out of corners with a grin and a butcher knife. I take it back. You could teach my mother a thing or two!''

"I didn't know bastards had mothers!" she snapped.

"You're transparent, Melissa. That kind of crack is calculated to drag me over there, teeth gnashing. You'd love that, wouldn't you, goading me into belting you one?''

"You make me laugh," she said. "*HA. HA.* You're like every other man. Emasculated by Mom! No interest in real flesh and blood women. Oh, no. That would be too real, too much for your puny mentality. What you want is an imaginary creature, either fighting you tooth and nail on a tiger skin or swooning on a bed of rose petals at the sight of you.

"Your ego is so warped, you need the constant assurance of being seen with a flashy chorus girl or a model. You get your jollies when you think other men are slobbering over your date, wishing they were in your shoes. You may be reasonably tall and reasonably good looking but you have the outlook of a short, fat skinhead with wet lips, clammy hands and a big fat cigar, surrounded by hot and cold running blondes hired by the hour!''

"You live with your neuroses," he said blandly, not looking at her. "I'll live with mine. Mine at least give me a few laughs. You, on the other hand, take

106

yourself *so-o-o* seriously. Populations are exploding, atom bombs are rubbing up against each other, Africa is writhing in the birth pangs of nationalism, yet you seem to think that all a man thinks about is sex and that when a man sees you all he can think about is flattening you on your back. Well, it may come as a shock but I think you should know there are other things in this world besides fornication, and men and women do occasionally find another area for mutual enjoyment. Your outlook has become so futile, so pointlessly narrow that you've boxed yourself in, turned off your brain and let your glands to the thinking. You've stopped functioning as a person—as a woman—except from the waist down!''

"Keep your armchair analysis to yourself. I'm not interested. Open your own head and look inside before you hand out any more free advice."

"Can we go to dinner now?" He stubbed out his cigarette.

"No—I think not," she said, wearied by combat. Passing up a free meal was a sign of maturity. "I think we've said all we have to say. Dinner would be anticlimatic, don't you think? Anyway, I'm not all that hungry."

At the door he turned, flushed with anger. "I'd like to reserve decision on your offer, Melissa. I'll try to find the time to sample the merchandise before making up my mind."

If Scotch weren't so expensive, she'd have flung the bottle at him. Instead, she kicked the door in her fury, an expression of temper from childhood. This time, however, the chiffon skirt impaired her aim and she rammed her toes, exposed by the flimsy sandals, into the wood molding.

She sat down in a heap, rubbing her foot and clenching her teeth against tears which would ruin her eye makeup. The luxury of crying would be cancelled out by the tedious process of taking off and putting on her face. If she were a dog, she would be able to lick her wound, but since infancy she had been unable to put her foot in her mouth—except figuratively, of course.

Feeling better at her own joke, she stood up, unzipped the dress and made herself a fat sandwich of the remaining liver paste. She drank three cups of black coffee while watching a mystery movie on TV, re-did her makeup anyway, changed into a pale blue jersey Ingrid had given her because it stretched in cleaning, and, fashionably late, went off to meet Dominic.

The doorman at El Morocco nodded vaguely as he opened the door. Doormen didn't recognize her, nor did headwaiters, saleswomen or others whose personal acknowledgement made the difference between insville and outsville. It gave her a creepy feeling of being invisible, like being introduced to the same person three times at a party and not being remembered.

Dominic dominated the bar, talking with his hands to a mocha-colored girl and a slate-gray man. She determined not to mention the eviction. Dominic couldn't care less, she was sure, and little would be gained playing the orphan unless she wanted to be adopted.

The two were, in order of rank, the Maharajah of Cooch-Poona and his traveling companion cum social secretary, Daphne Brooks-Hulme, an Anglo-Indian and one of the more beautiful if less permanent mementoes of British dominion.

Dominic and Coochie had shared digs at Magdalen in 1938 and after the war had strengthened a lifetime bond by trying to swim from Cannes to Corsica during a particularly jolly Riviera holiday. It was no race, mind you, nothing so coarse as that between gentlemen, merely a leisurely test of comdradely endurance such as strolling from London to Land's End, a popular Victorian pastime.

Friends in evening dress, standing on the Croisette, had watched them step out of their clothes on the beach and into the moon-dipped surf, calling out odds and making bets on the winner. When they disappeared from sight and showed no signs of returning, the still-hilarious party hired a speedboat and found them stroking in rare good form and barely winded. The mermen protested vigorously at being fished out. Corsica could not be far. Dominic fell into a champagne sleep, his head in the lap of a woman he had wanted to know better all evening. Coochie retched sea water all the way back, his grayish complexion all the more ashen for the moonlight and his condition.

"This is my glamorous American friend I've been telling you so much about—the only American girl in the entire continent with whom I can spend more than five minutes without going mad. Melissa Kempton."

Daphne nodded speculatively. Coochie said in clipped British accents, "How d'you do," his pudgy ring-rung hand like a living abacus studded with stones taking hers, his pudgier mouth bending to anoint it with a cigar-damp kiss.

"You are married, my dear?"

"Yes—that is, no . . ." she replied in confusion.

"Melissa is divorced," Dominic broke in. "It's a custom here in the colonies. Upon reaching puberty, young people marry at once to satisfy the curiosities of their flesh. Once the mysteries are uncovered, they have no further use for their mates and dispose of them, like an extra layer of skin."

"Ah yes, yes," Coochie examined her with the candor of a cartoon sheik shopping at the slave market for a harem replacement. "Charming, Dominic. Absolute heaven, dear boy. You won't be jealous if I give her my card? My card, Mrs. Melissa. When you are in the neighborhood, you must pop in for a few weeks. During the season there is always lashings of room and quite amusing company. You would be a *divertissement*."

The heavily-crested card gave the address of a villa in Portofino, Italy.

"Ah, yes," he said, "I am in virtual exile. My palaces and harems are gone. It is infinitely more politic that I function beyond the borders of my native soil."

"What a shame," Melissa said, looking to Dominic for guidance. But he seemed to be looking to Daphne for guidance.

"Would you care to dance, Miss American Beauty? My corpulence does not prevent my being facile with my feet."

"What brings you to New York?" Melissa asked brightly after one lap around the floor.

"Deep-freezes and refrigerators."

There was no reply but, "Oh."

110

"One cannot escape the dreary world of commerce any longer. Where once my chief concern would be the pleasure of horses and women, I must now supplement my income. I am a salesman. I have taken back a part of the white man's burden."

He shook soundlessly at the jest. "Civilization and self-rule have brought modern thought to my people. They want refrigeration and birth control in that order. So, to help my people I forego the pleasures to which rank entitles me, and wander the market places of the world, buying equipment for distribution by my agents in India and Pakistan. A bloody Wog, plain and simple."

"A Wog?" she said with dismay. "Isn't that a term of derision?"

"Not really, my dear. So long as one is referring to one's self. It's not a nasty word. When the first Indians became British civil servants and adopted European dress, they were called Wogs—Westernized Oriental Gentlemen. Very simple, and that's what I've become."

"But you're helping to modernize your country. That's what's so exciting," she said, gazing into his hot licorice eyes to make him feel better about being a Wog. It was a mistake. His chubby hand pressed into her back.

"Rubies? . . . Sapphires? . . . Rubies, I think. Yes . . . No . . . sapphires!" he crooned. "Sapphires are your jewel . . . strikingly cold and regal yet streaked with desire. You must allow me to present you with a sapphire, a tribute to your beauty."

She looked toward the bar for help and panicked. They were gone.

"I'm allergic to sapphires. They make me break out in a rash. It's grim. I once tried some on in Tiffany's and I had to have an injection."

"You American girls! So droll! Coming out in spots over sapphires! My dear, you shall have one for every finger—and a massive one for your navel as well."

Had Dominic dumped her, or cunningly traded her in to Coochie for that—that sari with the (Christ, what rhymes with fringe?) on top? Dominic pretended to no moral code but this was going too far.

"Tell me about Poona," she urged.

"You are delicious! So serious! So determined to stay out of my clutches. You ask for nothing so you shall have many gifts. And I shall even tell you about Poona. It is a lovely city situated southwest of Bombay on the westerly coast of the Arabian Sea . . ."

"You two have had quite enough fun. We want to cut in." It was Dominic and the hyphenated sari, pulling them apart.

"Dominic! Where have you been? I thought you'd skipped out leaving me with old baubles, bangles and beads. He wanted to plant a sapphire in my navel."

"Jolly good! I could see you'd hit it off. I'm so pleased. Of course we didn't bolt. Whatever for? We moved to a table. It's Coochie's party, by all means let's enjoy it. And don't worry, darling, I won't let anything nasty happen to your delicious navel."

As night turned to morning, Dominic and Daphne bent closer and closer to each other, leaving Melissa to chatter inanely with Coochie. By rough count he had given her four elephants, a Rolls-Royce, a chateau in the Dordogne and a racing stable.

From the way fire-water affected him, she wished

the Federal law against serving spirits to Indians also applied to East Indians.

She began to wonder which of the two men was her date. Or was she up for grabs? It was a chronic disease of Groupsville, symptomized by a vagueness about who was with who, or was it whom?

At the very moment Coochie began playfully to Indian hand-wrestle with her (although she was sure he didn't call it that) for silver dollars with which he had thoughtfully bankrolled her, Walter Simpson brushed past the table behind a redhead in white, head-turner first class.

He nodded without pausing and continued on. Melissa felt inexplicably embarrassed. The mad, gay International Set seemed suddenly shoddy in contrast to this cleancut if crazy mixed-up American man.

Fortunately, Coochie reeled to his feet and said, "I'm going to be ill," knocking over a bottle of Courvoisier enroute to the gentleman's. Minutes later they were herded into a waiting Rolls for the trek home. Too much hoochie for dear old coochie.

"Drop me first, Dominic, please. Daphne may need help getting him into bed and I'll only be in the way."

Alone in her bedroom, she double-locked the window to the balcony and pulled the blinds. That would keep old Romeo from returning for a second night's stand—an unlikely event from the look on Daphne's face.

Only five more nights to outsville. Something would save her. Something always did. A child of destiny. Asking Walter's help had been an idiotic mistake. She would never be so vulnerable again.

She feel asleep while trying to work out in her mind

113

whether she had chosen to sleep alone because of a fierce desire to somehow show Walter or because tonight's plot and cast of characters had jarred a slumbering self-respect.

Sleeping Beauty had awakened to reality because an aging Prince Charming had spit in her eye.

# SUNDAY

"WHAT CHANCE FOR ROMANCE AFTER SIXTY?"

"REVENGE OF A HAREM QUEEN!"

"THE DOG WHO SAVED A NATION"

"THE AMERICAN MALE—FREAK OR FOOL?"

Melissa rolled over on the Sunday supplements. Between "We Found Our Island Paradise" and "Is Divorce Sapping Our Economy?" she was very depressed.

The Sunday papers were gunning for her at every turn. Ads for clothes she couldn't buy. Travel stories about romantic trips she couldn't afford. Success stories about girls younger than she. Society chatter about people she knew by sight wearing the clothes that would look better on her at the faraway places that would assuredly bring happiness if she could only get there.

There were menus for dinner parties when your husband's boss was invited if you had a husband and decorating ideas for nurseries suitable for the child she could sometimes imagine straining inside her to escape.

Then there were the classified ads for GIRLS GIRLS GIRLS and WOMEN WOMEN WOMEN offering pleasant conditions, good pay, employee benefits. She wondered whether she still qualified as a GIRL or had graduated to WOMAN. When did the metamorphosis occur? In your sleep? The Help Wanted Male section didn't solicit BOYS BOYS BOYS. So far as industry was concerned, all BOYS were automatically MEN. How wrong they were. She would take her own ad. "MAN WANTED. Bright. Affectionate. Aggressive. Must be mature and an orphan."

The wedding announcements saddened her more than the obituaries. Troths plighted. Vows taken. Plans formalized, finalized, lionized. What about annual reports on nuptial partnerships? Business published reports on mergers, dividends, and new stock issues. Why not assess the wedding merger with evaluation of each partner's investment and the type of issue if any. Society page journalism should keep pace with the times.


### M. KEMPTONS

### RIFT ANNOUNCED

*special correspondent*
*The marital rift of Mr. and Mrs. Maxwell Kempton of this city has been announced joyfully by his mother, Mrs. Muriel Kempton. After an amicable divorce, the couple will remain in New York. Mrs. Melissa Kempton will retain her mar-*

*ried name because of all the monogrammed linen and stationery. She will be "At Home" practically all the time at the former nuptial residence on East 50th Street. Friends have been asked to omit flowers, send money.*

There were horoscopes and personality quizzes, all of which predicted a bright and sunny future provided she changed her entire point of view.

She read the book reviews, memorized the new titles and bogged down halfway through the crossword puzzle. In the entertainment section, she marked the plays, films and concerts she wanted to see. Little Miss Marker. Getting to see them would all depend on whom she could lure into taking her. Another drawback of Groupsville was that no one ever got together early enough in the evening to do anything except drink, talk and re-group. It was a self-protective device activated to forestall making a decision. Resistance to definite plans ruled unless tickets to an opening were dumped in your lap at the last moment. Then it was chic to be late.

Most depressing of all this lovely Sunday in June were the Apartments For Rent. There were one-room fifth floor walk-ups with pullman kitchens for more rent than she was paying now. There were elegant three-room penthouses with sunny terraces and doormen for about one-third the national debt. There were sublets with air-conditioning and valuable antiques, cooperatives to buy if she were really discriminating and a refined, middle-aged woman, Christian, renting part of her comfortable apartment with its own private entrance and kitchen privileges.

She decided to get up and have some coffee before

even getting up became too depressing and she pulled the pillow over her face to shut out the world completely, forever.

It was noon and the sun shone squarely on the street, caressing the facades on both sides equally with radiant heated hands. She unlocked the balcony window and stepped outside, idly wondering if Dominic had played the human fly again only to be thwarted by a lock. He was too much of a swashbuckler to knock and ask to be let in. Assault and conquer in one dashing spurt of bravado, or go away and come again another day, Melissa didn't want to play.

With summer, the Weekend Bit would begin. Jockeying for invitations from people with pools, beach footage or boats, preferably no children. As a divorcee with no known wealth and a good five years older than the usual extra girl invited to fill in a weekend party, she was a drug on the market.

Being invited on her own meant facing the possibility of some social misfit being provided as her date by a scheming hostess. Being invited by a man to a friend's retreat meant accepting him as a sleeping partner on anything from a raffia mat to a wonky hammock.

Packing was fraught with trauma because you were always at the mercy of plans never quite clear. An informal weekend might mean anything from faded levis to yards of chiffon at the country club. It wasn't chic to arrive with a trunk to cover all possibilities. She always threw in the red chiffon no matter what the hostess said. It needed no ironing and nine out of ten times she wore it.

Divert her mind as she might, the glaring fact remained as vivid as the sunshine. She had to be off this balcony, out of this house, away from this charming street in four days. Over and above the faded jeans and clinging chiffon, her packing must include everything. Pictures, books, household goods. The works.

Where to? And what then? Storage rates were so high she might as well stash herself away with the furniture. "I Call A Storage Warehouse Home."

Max would come this afternoon, she was certain. If he were in town and received her message, he would come and do something efficient. No matter what, she could always count on Max.

The phone had not rung once. Its silence made her nervous. Ingrid would still be asleep. She used Sunday as "Camel Day" to store up enough rest for the entire week.

Call Dominic? No. Let sleeping dogs lie. For once, a cliché fit.

Max? No. Talking on the telephone with him was so strained, so unrealistic. Communing with another planet, every word fraught with the danger of misunderstanding.

Being divorced, having an "Ex" to discuss was supposed to be sophisticated and fun. At least that was how it had seemed from inside the wedding ring. On the outside looking back in she saw the inner circle as confining, yes, but rimmed by a discernible border that established a geographic entity, a definite sphere inside the golden horizon. Outside was limitless space with millions of light years to the sun, a jillion orbits to join and the constant threat of colliding with another lost heavenly body and burning out before the accustomed cyclic conclusion.

Max would come at four. Of this she was certain. Max was reliable. Even when he was feeding her inch by inch through the meat grinder, he was with her all the way through, holding her hand, protective of her feelings. And when she came out the other end a shapeless mass of mincemeat he unfailingly tried to reshape her in the form of a woman.

Well, do something physical. Move the furniture around. Again, what was the use? In four days she would be moving it anyway—out! Unless somehow, somewhere, some thing could be done to forestall it.

She would clean the house. Work up a little honest sweat. Give the pores a party. Lella, the once-a-week maid, had been beaten senseless by her common-law husband and was recuperating happily in the hospital.

Her mother was right, of course. The house was a pigpen and she had behaved worse than a pig. Stepping back inside the bedroom, she dialled her mother's number, then quickly replaced the phone. *He* might answer. Anyway, a tearful reconciliation might bring Claire tearing over and the whole thing would begin again. Easier on all concerned to stay on the outs another few weeks, or at least until after the eviction business and getting resettled.

Let Claire badger Ellis and the grandchildren for a while. Ellis! She suddenly remembered that her sister, brother-in-law and two children were driving into town at about three, right after Mimsey's nap, to see an exhibition of ancient dolls at the Metropolitan Museum and have dinner at the Automat, the height of culinary adventure for the deep freeze generation.

Ellis had telephoned early in the week to say they would stop in and say hello if she were going to be

120

home. Melissa hadn't seen her nieces in months, not since the week after Easter when she had spent the night at their Levittown split-level while John attended a convention in Chicago.

She had helped Ellis clean and take care of the children, enjoying the pungent smell of furniture oil, the pleasant twinge of forgotten muscles, and the quiet relief of sipping coffee in the kitchen with her sister, re-establishing a bond that perhaps never existed.

To honor the impending arrival of Mr. and Mrs. John Claud Wilson and their enchantingly adorable daughters, Bethany Sue and Mimsey Ann, Melissa Jane would clean the house. AND hunt up some little gifts for the babies AND try to get along famously with John.

John disapproved of her, Melissa knew. He was uncomfortable, even sullen, in her presence and especially on her own stamping ground. His saturnine intolerance of her, his bird-like pecks—"How is the all-around postdeb?"—"What are you doing away from El Morocco? Do you need a passport to get in?"—"We're just simple suburbanites. We don't know how to live but we manage!"—had often goaded her into an extravagant counter-attack.

Once, just a few weeks after the divorce, he and Ellis dropped in for a drink before meeting some friends. "Well, tell me, Missy," he had said, "how does a glamorous divorcee operate? How do you get back into circulation so you can nab a richer one this time?"

With her sister's hush sounds in her ears and John protesting he was only making conversation, she had fled upstairs, slipped into a pair of leopard skin pants,

121

coated her eyelids purple and fished an absurdly long cigarette holder from a drawer of miscellany.

Preceded by the cigarette holder and a coil of hair over one eye she had slunk into the sitting room, eased herself into John's startled lap and purred in her Marilyn Monroe voice, "Here's how I go about getting a new man. You interested?"

Ellis had laughed uproariously, clasping her baby sister to her. "Remember the time we went to that party in our riding clothes and said we were in training for the Olympics?" The two giggled and recalled other shared moments while John sat and glared into space.

It was as if he were triumphant in her failure, as if I-told-you-so were written all over him since the divorce. He believed suburbia was the only atmosphere in which a family unit could flourish, regardless of how inconvenient to the husband. Couples living in the city were tempted by too many distractions. He contended, whenever the subject came up, that they spent their time being glamorous instead of building a life together.

He had encouraged Ellis to gain a few pounds and wear her hair comfortably in an unbecoming knot. A wife should look like a wife, not a fashion model. Ellis liked to eat and if John wanted long hair pulled back in a bun it was certainly easier and cheaper than dashing to the hairdresser's every week. Melissa thought John was afraid of having a glamorous wife. She hoped he wouldn't buy a new pair of glasses and hate the drab Galatea of his making.

What Melissa could not know was her sister's nightly enjoyment of having her husband take her hair down and fondle it as he eased her back against the

122

pillows with the tangled mass framing her soap-scrubbed face and the steady sound of breathing on the inter-com telling her the children were peacefully asleep.

She thought of cleaning the house naked, like stories she'd read of women in the mines. She got so dirty anyway, it seemed easier to cover herself with cleansing cream to catch the dust, tie her hair up in a scarf and then shower the filth away when it was all over. She compromised on an old bathing suit and a pair of torn gloves. Housework contributed very little to fingernails.

She hated rags, didn't know what to do with them once they got dirty. Washing them seemed so revolting. She solved the problem by throwing them away. On her knees in the kitchen she scrubbed the linoleum singing an old Negro worry song:

> Motherless children have a sad time
> When the mother is dead
> Motherless children have a sad time
> When the mother is dead
> They ain't got no place to go
> Gotta travel from do' to do'
> Motherless children have a sad time
> When the mother is dead . . .

Feeling as house-proud as Harriet Craig with hot pants she scrubbed herself last of all and after careful consideration of John and Ellis, donned a pair of tight black contour pants, a matching basque pullover that had shrunk in the laundromat and a scarlet scarf tied like a hair ribbon around her head. Sweet, serene and never been misssed.

No point in disappointing John.

She was looking forward to seeing Ellis. Most of their lives had been a series of arrivals and departures, Ellis at boarding school when their father died, pretending after the funeral that it hadn't happened while she answered the chatty letters from her mother and the piteous tear-splashed noted from Missy telling her about "that man." Melissa fiercely resented being abandoned by her sister who was not only away from home but wearing lipstick and having dates.

When Melissa's turn came, "that man's" finances were rocky so she went to Julia Richman, a public high school, while Ellis went on to college, graduating the year before her younger sister's entrance.

She remembered her first weekend at Ellie's shortly after Bethany's birth and before her own marriage. Max was away and she accepted Ellie's frequently offered invitation to see how the married people live.

Just back from a year in Europe, she had vowed not to country-drop or talk too much about night clubs and her exciting life in the outside world. She needn't have worried. Nobody had given her a chance to say much of anything.

All the women were immersed in children, homes and recipes. Their husbands were engrossed in lathes, hammocks and bowling scores. Each contingent spoke its own language. Neither went beyond, "So you're Ellie's sister?" She had left early on the Sunday, pleading an expected long-distance call from Max.

Would she have become this kind of woman if she had borne her baby? She doubted it. A bump in your

124

belly didn't sap your zest for clothes, your appetite for people and places. She would have been one of those sleek Moms with a copy of *Vogue* wrapped around the baby's bottle to insulate it. Her child would have sparkled with health and wit all day, slept without a murmur through the night and never bit anyone but grandma.

She didn't begrudge Ellis her evident happiness but it did honestly seem so dreary. Why couldn't marriage be gay and stimulating instead of stultifying? Discounting an evening like last night with Coochie and his creepy girl friend, the superficial life of kicks today and kicks tomorrow was preferable to bland respectability.

At five to three the station wagon debarked two little girls aged four and two, identically dressed in yellow lawn with blonde straw bretons and long streamers down their backs.

"Aunt Missy. Aunt Missy," they screamed. "Where's the Queen's Jewel Box?" Beth demanded. "Can we play with it again?"

Ellis waved from the curb where she was collecting their belongings while John locked up. They would leave the wagon there and proceed around town by taxi. Parking was a problem John was too sensible to tackle.

"Come, my charmers," she hugged both little girls and inhaled their sweetness. "I'll take you upstairs to the Queen's Dressing Room where we shall see Her Majesty's jewels and select one each—no more—for your very own."

She took off their hats and shiny patent leather shoes and set them in the middle of her bed. She had forgotten their game of the previous visit but children always remembered. With measured steps and imitating a trumpet, she brought them a large wooden casket filled with discarded junk jewelry she kept, meaning to give away. There were seashell necklaces, tarnished charm bracelets, single earrings, relics of past madness: a Zuni torquoise squash blossom necklace, a Mexican silver pendant, a Florentine enamel, an English horse brass that had fallen off a belt.

"If either one of you little monsters wants the bathroom, it's right there. No fair wetting anybody else's bed. Only your own!" she said with mock sternness, waving her finger in their faces.

Bethany laughed merrily at her aunt's warning and Mimsey joined in, not sure exactly why. She left them screaming over possession of a cat pin with one eye missing.

"Hi . . . what do you want to drink? Something cold? Beer? Seven-Up? Something stronger?"

Ellis threw herself onto the couch with a sigh of contentment. "Beer for me, baby. I've been up since three with goon girl number one. Nightmare. Being chased by an alligator dressed as a baseball player."

"With a bat? Uh, oh, Freudian symbol there!" She thought of Walter and flushed. "Gotta watch out. You'll have to buy a head-shrinker!"

Ellis laughed. "The hell with Freud. I think she saw an alligator in a comic book. Go get me that beer before I expire."

"And you, John? A beer, too?"

He had remained standing. "No, no thanks, Melissa," he said firmly. Then, turning to his wife, "Honey, you look bushed. Why don't I take the girls

126

to the UN while you have some girl-talk with your sister? I'll be back in half an hour and we can go to the museum from there. Beth's nursery school teacher told them about the UN building, showed them pictures of it and told them to ask their parents to take them to see it," he explained to Melissa.

"Why don't you sit down and relax and tell Beth to tell her teacher to—" she saw the expression on his face and stopped.

"Well," she continued jovially, "you can certainly have a quick beer before you go. The UN's just down First Avenue. It won't go away. The girls are very busy upstairs decking themselves out in my jewelry so you might as well relax for a moment."

Still standing, John accepted the beer and gulped it down. He called the children but Melissa finally had to go up and wrench them howling from the treasure chest, promising to leave everything as it was until they returned.

"What's a UN?" Mimsey asked as she was pulled backwards through the door.

Mother and Aunt laughed. "A lot of people older than she is have asked the same question."

"Out of the mouths of babes. She's adorable, Ellis. Couldn't be cuter. What's up? You knitting teeny garments again?"

"Why, no . . ." Ellis blushed. "I guess I am getting a little plump, Melissa. It's so hard to keep thin. With the girls and the housework and driving around so much I never seem to take time for a balanced meal except at night. Just coffee breaks with sandwiches and doughnuts or whatever's handy on the run. John

127

keeps telling me he likes me this way, but maybe I shouldn't listen to him.''

''He's the only person you should listen to, your own husband. He loves you very much. He's given you two babies. And you love him.''

''Yes, baby, I do. We've been married seven years and we live in a madhouse of meals, toys, running noses and crayon in the drains but I still feel like a bride sometimes.''

''That's wonderful, Ellis. Hang onto it. I'm so happy for you.''

She sat at her sister's feet observing the sensible shoes that squared her ankles, the dumpy skirt that squared her hips, the too-large blouse that rounded her shoulders and the absence of makeup that blurred her features. Just a touch of pencil or her near-blonde eyebrows would strengthen the expression.

As Ingrid was to Melissa, Melissa was to her sister. ''I have just the scarf to jazz up that shirt,'' she said, hauling Ellis up from her comfortable position. ''Come on up to my boudoir . . .'' she said, twirling an imaginary mustache. ''Even my etchings have etchings.''

''Ohhhhh,'' Ellie moaned, struggling to her feet. ''No peace for the wicked. Have you no respect for motherhood?''

That was a laugh.

Ellis enjoyed her sister's dressing room and the jungle of artifice as much as her children. She felt no sibling rivalry. Their paths had never crossed in war except for the usual destruction of each other's belongings as children. They had never poached each other's boy friends or fought for the affection of their parents. Ellis had stumbled into a marriage she found completely satisfying and she viewed with affectionate indulgence Melissa's turbulent search for expression and with deep anxiety her sudden divorce and insularity in the ensuing year.

Defensive in a way about her own happiness, aware of its none-too-apparent values and rewards in her sister's eyes, she could not stifle a momentary envy of this house, Melissa's flair for fashion, the trips abroad, the idle chatter about El Morocco and other places she had never been.

John had been her first and only lover. If there were better, she didn't know about them or care. He satisfied her in every way as much as she believed a woman could be satisfied. Yet, at times she wondered about Melissa's travels and the European men she must surely have known intimately. She confined these flights of fancy to day-dreaming while making up meat pies in quantity for her freezer storage.

"I have something to tell you," Melissa kept her tone light but her eyes said it was serious.

"You're getting married! You're going back to Max! What is it? Tell me!"

"Nothing as glamorous as orange blossoms. I'm being evicted. Do you think I should send out an announcement? Maybe someone will give me a shower."

"But when? Why? Where will you live?"

"Oh, it's been hanging over me like Damocles' sword for about six months. The house has been sold from under me. The new owner wants to put up a bordello with bowling alleys or something. They've asked me very politely to leave several times. Now, they're playing rough. A man came with a piece of paper yesterday and it's outsville. I have to clear the campus by Thursday."

"Four days to pack up this lovely house?" Her own split level never seemed more secure. "What will you do? Have you found another apartment? If you want me to drive in with the station wagon to help, I'll dump the kids with a neighbor."

"I may just become a white slave! There's nothing else for me. There weren't any decent apartments in the classified ads. I'll probably move in with Ingrid if all else fails. In the meantime I'm trying to pull strings to get a stay of execution. You know I believe in miracles."

"Well, you certainly don't want to move in with mother and 'that man'." Despite being married to their mother for more years than their father he could not escape the reference.

"No. But don't tell Mother about this at all. I don't want her getting hysterical until it's all over."

Ellis nodded and took her hand. "I know how you feel about suburbia and all but if you ever, for any reason, even if it's just to save on rent, want to stay with us for a few weeks, we'll fix up the playroom and keep the girls out of it so you can have privacy. Anytime, Melissa. You can count on me."

Big Sister was watching her. She had no choice but to look grateful. To stay with her sister and the Great Silent One would signify defeat more than moving to the Y or in with Ingrid which at least kept her in the Manhattan whirlpool.

"Thanks, Ellis. That's sweet of you. Maybe I will. Or at any rate, maybe I'll dump some of my belongings on you for safekeeping. Look around while you're

130

here. If there's any furniture you can use, put a mark on it. Max is coming over later. He gets first choice being as he's the one who paid for them. I thought it was only fair.''

"Max coming?" Ellis searched her sister's face. "Do you see him often?"

"No! Why should I see him?" She busied herself with the items on her dressing table. She picked up the container of cotton and dropped it with a shriek.

"What's the matter?" Ellis started. Max couldn't be giving her the screams.

"Blood. There's blood on that cotton!" It had seeped through the sock after all. "I—I cut myself yesterday." (And killed Max's mother.)

"Is that all? I didn't think you were squeamish about a little blood. With a family you get used to it. Between their noses, their knees and their elbows I could start a blood bank.''

She pinched off the speckled bit of cotton and threw it away. "There, there, naughty cotton all gone now."

She paused to consider how she might say the next words. "Seriously, Melissa, I think your nerves are shot. You need to put your life on an organized footing. Maybe a regular job is the answer—to give you a routine to follow. I know how you've always carried on against routine, against the restrictions of working for other people, fitting in with their whims and moods. You want to lead your own life, but leading it depends on other people. You're not a hermit. You're a social animal but you need a milieu for communicating with people besides the dry martini and . . .''

". . . and money, Ellis. Mustn't forget money."

131

"And money, sure, and a means of expressing your-self."

"What you're trying to say is that I'm a misfit and not good enough to be a successful free-lance."

"No—what I'm saying is free-lancing is a lonely life. You can't spend your so-called free time—which far from being free is damned expensive to you—meeting your friends and sleeping late. Even if you could afford it, the fruitless squandering of time and energy can get you down. How long since you've made some ceramics?"

"Quite a while," Melissa said, declining to admit not since the divorce.

The kiln had been the hub of her creativity. Would Walter call that a womb, too, a hot oven for the trans-formation of human-molded clay into living artistry? She had found serenity and sensual contentment in throwing the clay of the wheel and feeling the shape form as the rotating glob moved cold and wet to the gentle guidance of her hands.

Gradually, the pliant mass became a cone, narrow-ing and narrowing, taller and taller, spirals of ridges made by an indiscernible pressure of thumbs or mus-cle. The final shape was completely in her hands. She was at once omnipotent creator and humble apprentice with much to learn.

"And it looks like it will be quite another while when I move from here. You can't exactly set up a kiln in a one-room apartment."

"Anybody ho-o-o-o-me . . ." Beth and Mimsey chorused from the street.

"Back so soon," Ellis muttered, taking off the pais-

132

ley ascot and tooled leather belt and starting downstairs dressed as she had come up.

"They complained there was nothing to see at the United Nations," John explained, smiling. "No hot dog stands or kiddie rides is what they mean."

"When are we going to see the dolls?" Beth demanded, jumping up and down, the jewel box forgotten.

"Right now, honey," Ellis slung her strap pouch over one sloping shoulder. It contained tissues, sweaters, a box of animal crackers and other oddments vital to outings with children.

"Hello, Uncle Max. Where've you been!?" A delighted Bethany broke from the group in front of the door and dashed down the street toward the approaching visitor.

Much embarrassed by the encounter, Max completed his journey with a triumphant Beth straddling one hip. Mimsey clamored to be hoisted up, too.

"How are you, Ellis . . . John . . . Melissa? Nice day."

"You're looking well," Ellis observed, unhooking her children. "Come on, girls, the dolls are waiting for us."

"But we want to see Uncle Max," Beth wailed. She liked men. Took after her aunt, Ellis always said to John's annoyance.

"Uncle Max has come to see Auntie Melissa, not us," she said, grinning conspiratorily. "And if we're going to go to the Automat later we have to hurry."

"How many nickels can I have?" Beth was diverted.

"As many as you need," John scooped her up onto his shoulder and the caravan hit the westward trail.

Max had been fine until he turned the corner. Now he was uneasy. Melissa had always made him feel uneasy, a condition he had initially attributed to being in love. That outfit she was wearing made him uneasy, too, the tight pants and sweat shirt showing every curve. The outfit and the way she kissed him hello as if the divorce were just a broken date. Too aggressive. Never giving him a chance to find the curves for himself. Always on display.

"I got your message," he said, standing uncertainly in the sitting room he had signed away.

All the raillery died in her throat. She knew he hated what she was wearing, recognized now that she had known it earlier and willfully dressed that way in petty defiance. This was not going to be easy.

"Max . . . I won't bore you with small talk or sentiment. I'm being evicted. The house has been sold. I have to be out by Thursday."

They hadn't seen each other since a chance meeting on Fifth Avenue a few days before Christmas. They had had a civilized for-old-times-sake drink and he had kissed her in the taxi taking her home in the early dusk. If he had followed her inside, broken down the door of her cave instead of waiting to be asked . . .

"I'm sorry to hear that, Melissa. I know how much you like this house. Sometimes I used to think you married me for my house."

"Max!"

"I'm sorry, Melissa. Being here distresses me. Being an efficiency expert, I hate to think of all that

134

wasted time and effort. Now—the problem at hand. You're being thrown out so I assume you've investigated all the legal avenues of appeal and delay.''

She nodded.

''Well, then. What, exactly, do you expect me to do? Prove my manhood by finding the new owner and punching him in the nose?''

Faced with it, she didn't know what she expected from him. It was hardly fair to seek help from a husband she had dumped and on whom she had no moral or legal claim.

''Don't bear down on me, Max.'' It was hard to be helpless in that provocative outfit and also because Max knew her too well. ''I only wanted to let you have whatever furnishings you might like before I sell them or store them or give them away. I've been caught off balance with this, Max. It's not easy to simply pack up and move on like an Arab.''

''I sympathize with you,'' he said. ''I did it myself from these very surroundings.''

(He could always turn supplication to his own advantage.)

Walking around the sitting room as if it were a furniture store, he fingered the merchandise, ashtrays, books, a lamp here, a cigarette box there. ''To begin with . . .'' he pulled out a small leather bound note pad. ''Why don't I make a list as we go along? Make it easier for you to remember.''

She nodded mutely. Unwilling to help, he was happy to pillage.

''Let's see now,'' he rummaged. ''These Jane's Fighting Ships and my Greek myths and I've always liked this lamp and the chess table would fit into my apartment . . . now, remember, Melissa, if you change your mind or find another apartment real quick, you can have these things. I just don't want strangers to have them. Where are you planning to live in the meantime?''

"With Ingrid.''

He did not like Ingrid.

"You still have this I see,'' he said, holding the ceramic figure Calvin had admired.

"Yes,'' she said. "I think it's the best thing I've ever done.''

"I suppose it is,'' he said bitterly. "Its ungainliness is the perfect embodiment of your substituting art for me.''

"It is ungainly,'' she said, enunciating each word separately, "because it is a woman who happens to be *pregnant*!''

He slammed his hand down on the table. "Let's deny ourselves the pleasure of going into that again, if you don't mind.''

"Why not go into it? Why not! You called me a goddess once and a goddess can create things in her own image, can't she? The image of myself as I wanted to be, as I could have been, with a baby growing bigger and bigger inside of me and making me nauseous and lumpy and ungainly. Maybe, if you had let our baby live long enough I might have become too big to get up and down that narrow staircase. I could have spent the last few weeks upstairs on the chaise in our bedroom, Elizabeth Barrett With Child! This figure is my penance, Max, my memorial to something that never lived—our baby and our marriage!''

He braced himself as if in pain. "Melissa,'' he said

136

quietly, "this is old and bitter ground. I am, and was, a conventional man with a conventional outlook on marriage and child-bearing. A baby born three months after the wedding is hardly a sound beginning for either the child or the marriage!"

"The three month gestation period has become very popular the last few years," she parried.

"Only in those high café society circles you find so rewarding where the women change husbands and psychiatrists once a year with their automobiles and can't remember their children's names."

"There was nothing to stop our elopement and giving the baby an honest pregnancy!" The old argument. The crux of their estrangement.

"Why rehash it now, Melissa? Why torture yourself and me?"

"Because I live with it every day. I live with it when I see little children playing in the park, when I hold Bethany and Mimsey in my arms, when I look at my breasts in the mirror and know they were made for suckling, not just holding up a strapless bra. Because you couldn't overcome the fact that wedding invitations had gone out and your mother was giving us a dinner party and might be shocked to find out you conceived a baby without asking her permission. All the petty details of a wedding were more important to you than your own child!"

"If you will think back calmly, you will remember that you finally agreed with me, that we owed it to our parents—despite your vendetta against your mother and step-father—to give them the pleasure of a splashy wedding and all the nonsense that goes with it."

"Yes, I remember. I agreed because you were the

137

man and the man is supposed to be smarter than the woman. Maybe we should have been really practical and moved the wedding ahead two or three years so our baby could have been the flower girl or the ring-bearer! Maybe I would have had twins. Think of the beautiful wedding portrait that would have made!''

All the hatred and disappointment of the past few years gushed to the surface. ''You weren't worried about me! Or my insides! Or how I might feel about killing the most precious thing that can happen to a man and woman who love each other. You were worried first and foremost about your sanctimonious mother. What the old harridan would say if she knew. It was bad enough when she caught us sleeping together, wasn't it? You had failed her and her saintly morality. If she had found you with a whore that would have been okay, her healthy, strapping son refreshing himself with a lower animal! But to sleep in the arms of a woman who loved you and wanted to please you and cherish you and make you inexpressibly happy—*that* was dirty and disgusting and she made you promise not to do it anymore, you naughty boy, until the wedding night!''

''According to custom, couples should not sleep together until they are married.''

''According to whose custom? According to old deflated bags who've never known passion and desire and can't stand anyone else having it! Wearing that white dress was more sacreligious than getting pregnant, which had the virtue of being an honest mistake. The white dress was a travesty of purity, a mockery of us both, Max. Our marriage was over before it even began.''

138

Max sighed deeply. Perhaps he would take none of the furnishings, no reminders of the past. Soon the house would be in other hands or disappear entirely. He had stopped saving souvenirs at an early age. Yet, there were things he loved in this room, inanimate objects that did not vary, that could be counted upon to remain where and as he wanted them, give or take a little dust.

He wanted more than anything to escape. From this house. From her haunted eyes. He returned to his notebook. "This ashtray is a favorite of mine. Must hold a ton of butts. And I have a small terrace so if you don't want that little table in the garden and the two chairs, I'll take them."

He closed the notepad. "Well, I guess that does it." He did not want to go upstairs and stir his memory about furnishings or anything else. "Let me know where you'll be, Melissa. I'll continue to have your checks deposited in your account as usual."

He was leaving. He had just come and now he was leaving and nothing had been solved. By some magical alchemy she had hoped he would appear and drastically alter the situation, the Prince Charming who'd come to her with a charge account instead of a charger. The man of action whose idea of action was to light a cigarette.

As always, in an ever downhill slide from the peak of their love and the erosion of his mother's influence, he was letting her down.

Max sensed her thoughts, knew he was failing her. He could not remember when he did not feel an obscure sense of failure in her presence.

"You're doing it again—making me feel inadequate—and why the hell should I feel that way?"

"It's not my fault you're ineffectual. I wanted you to be my lord and master, to run our lives, to love me and protect me and let me be all the things a woman should be to her man—a servant, a courtesan, a hostess, a companion, a homemaker. I especially did not want to be your pal! And neither am I a matriarch. That's your mother's department. I'm surprised she lets you wear pants at all. If she could, she'd keep you in dresses and curls like that picture of your father she keeps on the piano."

He lost control of his equanamity then. She had finally reached him. "You blame everything on mother," he yelled. "The Mother Figure! My Mother! Your Mother! You have a morbid preoccupation with the subject. The whole of society emasculated by Mother! Next you'll blame the state of the world on the president's mother—or Stalin's mother!"

"I'd probably be right! If Czar Nicholas' mother had brought him up right he'd have made social reforms and there never would have been a revolution. The revolution was against Mother Russia!"

"You could go on a lecture tour with that one," he said, sarcastically. " 'Blame Mom For The Red Menace!' You accuse me, but you're the one with the Mother Fixation. You're the one with the crying need to be mother of the universe, make everyone play their role according to *your* preconceived ideas. Choosing the secondary role for yourself as my slave, my harlot, my plaything doesn't take you out of the driver's seat!

"You're trying to run the show and deluding yourself you're being a mere submissive woman! That's why I can't make love to you!"

"Make love to me!" she sneered. "You can't be a man. You can't even be an animal. Love? It isn't loving you can't do, it's another word, another four-letter word that you can't even say! A simple, crude four-letter word that you're afraid to say out loud."

"How many times . . . how many times," he was ranting, impervious to any sound but his own venom, "how many times did you allow me to make the supreme sacrifice in three years of marriage? You can count them on one hand! That supercilious look, that 'perform now, MAN and show WOMAN how virile you are and why you, MAN, are the superior sex!' That patronizing 'you can do it if you try, clumsy one' as if I were learning to ride a bike. Well, let me tell you something. You're wasting your time hating my mother. You're the most overpowering Mom of all! You hand out the chores and you give out performance awards!"

"Max! SHUT UP! I won't listen. You think sex is dirty like your mother does. Before we were married it was okay because we were being immoral, but afterwards—ah, afterwards, I was too respectable, too holy, too much in the same category as your mother. You couldn't sleep with your mother!"

Brutally, he gripped her shoulders. "Now you shut up!"

"You promised to make me pregnant again," she sobbed. "You held my hand and kissed my tears and promised me. But you didn't! You couldn't!"

"Because you tore off my balls!" he snarled close to her face. "But I've fooled you, Melissa. I am a man of the twentieth century with Miracle Testes and I've grown them back! I wrote an essay of twenty-five words on why I wanted them back and I won. I'm not letting you or any woman like you close enough to castrate me again.''

"Except your precious mother," she whimpered. "I can never forgive nor forget what you and your mother did to me . . ."

"My mother had nothing whatever to do with it. She knew nothing about it, then or now."

"It. *It*. Another word you're afraid to say. I quite agree with you, Max. Abortion is an ugly word. Some of the gals say they're having their appendix out and buy themselves a new dress as a post-operative pick-me-up. Not me. I don't feel that way about babies. I only remember a rubber mask over my face and, afterwards, seeing the bloody mess in the garbage can that the nurse forgot to cover. I bent over and looked at it, Max, our child, dumped in a garbage can!''

He had never allowed his mind to dwell on the physical realities of her visit to the New Jersey shore. He had sheltered in his own concept of a cheery white house, a shot in the arm, an overnight sleep and back again as good as new. Nothing more serious than a tooth extraction. The physical realities of childbirth distressed him. He could not imagine himself in an emergency situation delivering a baby such as policemen and taxi drivers supposedly did every day.

"I'm going now," he said. "I'll make arrangements to have the things picked up. When you're ready to move, have the movers send the bill to me."

She picked up the figurine with both hands and held

it to her face, breathing deeply against mounting hysteria. Ars longa. Amor brevis.

At first she had substituted art for love, as Max had accused. Then, when art wasn't enough she had discovered kicks.

She remembered her first cold-blooded experiment in extra-maritalia two years before. Her day had begun in the usual way, immersed in the tub, body proud as the hot water pinkened her skin and coated it with the slippery shine of wetness. The tub wasn't long enough for her. In order to straighten her legs, she propped them up against the end wall on either side of the faucets. She could turn the faucets with her toes, a far more practical party trick than picking up a pencil.

The bedroom beyond seethed with impatience. A man waiting for a woman. Let him wait, let him wonder, let him wait. She wallowed in the sublimity of inflicting torment. Love had gone down the drain one morning with the bath water. All that remained was flirtation and cheating and tricks. Staying in the water, pretending not to hear the anxious footsteps, the restless movement beyond.

He could stand it no longer. "Hey, you mermaid. Come on out of there. I only have an hour." His voice was boyish, eager, too eager. "I'm coming in to get you."

The door flew open. He stood there, warm and wanting and needing. He knelt and kissed her. He reached into the water, wristwatch forgotten, and scooped her up like a child on a sitdown strike in the wading pool. She allowed herself to be carried without the expected shrieks and protests.

Curiosity. Disintegration. Incipient decay.

"I'm sorry about last night, Melissa," Max had said, drying her with a large striped towel.

"Oh, it's all right, Max. Happens to the best of men. Maybe you're working too hard," she had answered consolingly, the visiting nurse who soothed the same plaints how many times.

"After all, you're not a machine. I don't put a nickel in you and expect you to function like an automaton. We're old married people now. It's all right, Max. Really . . ."

"No, it wasn't all right . . . and I'm going to make up for it right now." His ardor reminded her of their first passionate weeks in this room when the bed was a box spring on wooden blocks and he never unpacked his laundry but took the clean shirts as he needed them from the carton on the floor.

"I love you, Max," she whispered, trying to believe it, begging him to give her proof. He couldn't. Limp with failure, white with disgrace and a self-hatred beyond disgust, he left for the office.

Had "I love you" immobilized him? Did wanting a man emasculate him? The martyrdom had burned out. The comfort station was closed down for repairs. No more brave smiles that hurt him as much as her. Was she indeed the Great Emasculator or should she secede from the union?

Before she could decide, Rolland Slinger had called, asking if she were free for lunch. He had the hots for her, she could tell, or why else would he call? Perhaps she would toy with Mr. Slinger, an Iowa farmboy with a seat on the Exchange. It might help her morale to titillate Rolly, later to be known as Fall Guy Number One.

144

In retrospect he was very much like Martin, in a way. He liked to bring presents. There it was. The old refrain, "Can I bring anything?" his voice trembling with excitement.

"Yes—a bottle of Scotch. Maybe some black caviare or a Pont l'Eveque." Let him buy out the Vendome. "We can have lunch in and a long conversation."

Unless she changed her mind before noon, Rolly was in for a red letter day, her first misstep, the honeymoon long since having been *fini*.

Some faint scent she exuded must have reached him that morning all the way down on Wall Street. He rarely called anymore. She and Max had met him several months before at a cocktail party and their conversation had been so spontaneous, he had asked Max's permission to take her to lunch. After that they had talked on the phone a few times and that was all. His interest flattered Melissa, led her to extravagances of speech and manner to perpetuate his idolization of her as a glossy sophisticate.

Today he would find a fantasy come true. He had told her he admired nice feet on women so she painted her toenails orange and slid into a pair of tapered white trousers that hugged her like an ankle length girdle and a white sweater on her bare skin, no underwear, the better to see every crease, like the starlets on the Via Veneto.

If she were going to seduce him, it might as well be dramatic. She was realistic about her appetites after two fruitless encounters with Max in less than twelve hours. The spirit willing was all very well. Meaning well was all very well, too, but not enough.

Very well!

145

In a sudden panic, she rushed to the phone. Too late. Mr. Slinger had already left for lunch. He was not expected back until late. Was there any message? No.

Mr. Slinger could believe neither his eyes nor his obvious good fortune. For an Iowa farmboy, he had some unusual ideas. The white costume enthralled him.

"Turn around." He examined her minutely, like a dealer searching for flaws in the texture of a statue.

"Hope you don't mind, young lady. I've brought some salad things, too."

She stood motionless as he unpeeled the white covering and coated her with a film of olive oil. "Hope you won't mind, young lady. I always think of you as a great big bronze statue from a Greek temple gleaming in the sunlight. I've been wanting to see you this way. You're a damned good sport."

She pulled down the shades and served him his gourmet lunch. It was an amusing divertissement, a Romanesque charade. She was surprised only at her own lack of shame or modesty. Far from feeling wildly driven to depravity, she was strangely disembodied, watching herself with bored, cynical acceptance.

*Max—you've robbed me, cheated me. It's all your fault.*

Unusual as the preliminaries were, Rolly's next move was true to ritual, his anticipation almost ludicrous. By choice, Melissa was the cruel, inscrutable being, he the acolyte making obeisance to an idol of lust.

He tried to carry her. She was too heavy and didn't want to be carried. He worried about the oiliness on

146

her sheets. Nothing else on them, God knows, she spurred herself on.

She knew by instinct the pattern of the ritual, the movements and gestures which stirred the seeker to heights of worshipful ecstacy. After the proper amount of ceremony, she gave herself over as a pagan love sacrifice to an unborn ruler, to be ravished yet rise unblemished from the carnage. A phoenix.

She would die and live again, electrocuted, shot through with a million bolts man voltage, an electric shock treatment to purge her of all romanticism and jolt her back to reality.

*Oh, Doctor—I thought you'd never come.*

When he left, she had thrown up.

There had been others, though none so imaginative as Rolland. When Max refused her first request for a divorce, she had told him about them and left for Nevada.

The intervening time had proved nothing except that there were a lot of very talented men around willing and able to demonstrate their proficiency. Why not Max? Why couldn't they have had in the comfort and privacy of their home the cheap commodity to be found in drive-in movies, back roads and hotel rooms?

Rolland had been her first adultery. Melissa collected "firsts," savored them in times of reassessment, reviewed them instead of counting sheep the nights she couldn't sleep. President and Recording Secretary of the "First Men Who——Club." They included the first man who bought her a hot-dog, the first man who touched her breasts, the first man to buy her a present, the first man she ever saw naked.

The first man who kissed her armpit, the first man

147

who yelled at her, the first man who threatened to kill himself, the first man who bought her a diaphragm, the first man who made her think, the first man who made her cry, the first man who made her come.

The world was full of first men and the list would grow. Later, it might include the first man young enough to be her son, the first man she had to pay, the first man to laugh in her face, the first man to call her by the wrong name, the first man to have no face, no name, identity at all.

Even now, she could go to a party or stroll into Michael's or P.J. Clarke's and casually greet many of the members of her club. Many knew each other but none knew about the club or the bond each had with its president.

As always, the telephone rang.

Max?

Calvin. "Your voice sounds funny, Melissa. You crying?"

"No—it's nothing. I must have conked out. Did the Maharajah bit last night at Elmer's. Exhausted. How's everything with you? All settled? Quentin behaving?"

"Well, not exactly. Hey . . . can I come over and talk? You always tell me to call first so I'm calling. Who else can I turn to? You're almost like a mother to me, Melissa."

"I'm not ANYBODY's mother!" she shouted and slammed down the receiver.

# MONDAY

*I went to the rock to hide my face*
*And the rock cried out, "No hiding place!"*

Melissa planted her feet wide apart for balance on the buckled rubber matting that ran the length of the cross-town bus. On either side all she could see was the hostile rock of canyon walls, scarred by time and pigeons, bleak and forbidding to the melancholy traveler seeking a safe passage through.

*And the rock cried out, "No hiding place!"*

Nature provided camouflage for the beasts. For humans, there was no protective coloration. Not in the golden glare of marriage nor the blinding exposure of divorce. Nor the quagmire of a job. Nor the halo of sweet charity.

Politics?

Boresville united!

Give them back the vote!

Suffer ye women with your suffrage. Hatchets and

149

chains, force feeding and forced marches were a substitute for sex.

Take back the vote, and give us a seat in the bus!

Alcohol then?

Rye made her cry. Whiskey made her frisky. Gin made her sin. Scotch-on-the-rocks cried out like the Jubilee hymn, "No hiding place down here."

The house?

The house had been her shelter, her private cave in a city of caves. The last of the red-hot hiding places with a life expectancy of three days.

Hobbies?

Now *there* was oblivion. You were supposed to have hobbies because shorter work days and push-button homes left all that free time and it was un-American to just sit around and do a lint-count on your navel. Melissa's work day was so short, it was virtually non-existent. The utopian ultimate of leisure.

Free time was a misnomer.

It was very expensive. It was cheaper to work. That way you avoided the mental and financial taxations of guitar lessons, woodcraft, gourmet cookery and other self-improvements that only hastened the cycle of earn-spend-earn.

Actually there *was* one place to hide. Melissa knew it well. Fled to it often. Sex. It was better than working. It was cheap. You didn't need lessons or costly equipment you might never use again or a Master's Degree to assemble the parts. It was the last snug harbor of repose. Habit-forming, to be sure, but not destructive to the body like drugs or drink or over-eating. The only danger was progressive immunity. The glands refusing to respond. The reflexes dulled to the stimulus. The flesh crying out for more, more, more. The last door slowly closing.

She was not alone in her discovery of the last hiding place. Sex with a small or capital S, had become the leading leisure activity. For some, it was good politics, for others an engrossing hobby. To paraphrase the old lament, there was so little to do and so much time that, in a climate of glandular freaks in show business and circus performers in café society, the pursuit of love was running neck and neck with the pursuit of the buck.

As the bus caromed through the morning traffic, Melissa scanned the ad placards. A band of gypsy artists had evidently been at work with such native art tools as pencil and lipstick. Bra loveliness was crudely enhanced with the artist's x-ray concept of what lay underneath. An Over-28 Club blurb was brazenly inscribed with the writer's boast that he could do it over thirty times and didn't need a club. The Refined Hotel at Reasonable Rates had attracted a free spirit who had circled one window and scribbled, ''Hello, Goofball, wherever you are!''

There was something for everybody at eye level. Except for her. No discreet announcement for Nymphomaniacs Anonymous. No dignified phone number to call at a bad moment so they could send you a big strong eunuch to hold you in his arms until you were over the hump of late dates and charming luncheons at home.

Travel was so educational. She looked at her companions. There were ashen girls, minutes out of bed, struggling toward time clocks with their hair in pin curls under wrinkled bandanas and granules of sleep on their lids. There were serious young men in $50 copies of $200 suits, their lunch in an imitation leather attaché case and the *Times* folded to the financial section. There were the non-combatants, neatly impervious to in-fighting, reading the tabloids.

Then there were the chic young women. The secretaries and clerks trying to look like models by making up their eyes and carrying hat boxes. The models looking like models and not caring a damn but secretly pleased to be stared at. The girl fridays and junior executives, groomed with lacquered skill that meant getting up an hour earlier.

This morning she was one of THEM, the thundering herd she pretended to dispise. Yet, this clean-smelling morning, caught in the rhythm of a city going to work, she wished she were really a part of it, on her way to a niche that was hers among people who would miss her if she didn't turn up.

Bill Butler had asked her to stop by at 9:30 for a little talk. Obviously he was an insomniac. Nobody wanted to talk at that hour except to say "I love you" or "Give me a cigarette."

Clothes said more than a resumé if you knew how to choose them. Ingrid had taught her that. Today she was a combination of Bertha Business and Flora Fashion, a glossy machine, functional and decorative, for hire at so much an hour.


"Is it Miss or Mrs. Kempton?"

"Mrs."

"I'll be frank with you. I'm leery of married women in responsible positions. They all go pregnant on me."

152

"You'll have no problem there, Mr. Butler. I'm divorced."

"Well, that's how the ball bounces!"

She winced. That would cost him another five dollars.

"This office has been asked by a large department store chain to analyze women shoppers in twenty-five key cities."

He was a talker. Good. Chin on hand, she prepared to look intelligent.

"Our job will be to find out what they like and what they don't like about department store shopping. What extra services they would like to have. Whether the new fashions are put on sale too early or too late for them. For instance, some cities buy their Easter outfits in January. Others rush out the Saturday before Easter Sunday. We're looking for someone who looks like you. Young. Attractive. But old enough to be traveling by yourself. You will develop a questionnaire, contact women's groups in each city and pay a good-will call on the local store executives. They'll think you're a spy so they'll roll out the red carpet."

He was talking as if she had the job. They always did that. Twenty-five cities and all women! It was too depressing for words so early in the day.

"My fashion experience is not all that extensive," she said. The soft sell. Give the impression of knowing more than she was prepared to admit.

"Yes, but—" (He rose to the bait.) "That's exactly why you might be ideal. The woman we want likes clothes, has a few peeves of her own against department stores. A dyed-in-the-wool fashion expert is exactly what we don't want!"

Because they're too expensive, she thought. The dilettante might yet survive. She supposed she could stand the grating sound of women's voices for a few months. It would give her time to view her life in New York from a distance and work out her future role in the big city.

"It sounds like a fun job," she said. (About as much fun as root canal.)

"You'll be traveling most of the time, which is rough. But you'll have the best accomodations, a generous wardrobe and liberal expenses. Most of your salary will be gravy."

This might be the hiding place. An airplane seat with plenty of free coffee and a constantly changing view.

"If I may be crass, how much gravy?"

"In the neighborhood of $250 a week."

This was not a bad neighborhood for someone whose only other job had paid a fast ninety-five bucks. With Max's check, she would be in the upper brackets. This was not what she had hoped for but things rarely were. She had wanted a free-lance job, something glamorous and undemanding that paid well and enabled her to sleep late in the morning. Fairy Godmother? Where the hell were you?

She was definitely interested. In the money. The clothes. The legitimate excuse to leave New York on a glamorous expedition, far away from the Dominics and Calvins and Martins and Walters and especially, the house. After six months, she would have enough money to quit and go to Europe and Mr. Butler could find himself another amateur to exploit.

"Your project interests me strangely," she said.

"Would you be able to start Monday?"

"Yes."

As simple as that. She had changed her way of living with one word. Getting married required two words. "I do." Getting divorced was completely inarticulate. This was in between.

"Good." His voice became professionally sincere. "Now, I'm sorry it has to be this way but I have two more people to see, both recommended very highly. By some miracle, one of them might turn out to be more suitable than you. I doubt it but I have to be fair. If you can see your way clear to bear with me, I can let you know one way or the other by Wednesday."

See her way clear? She had already spent her first month's salary. Men were snakes. Lead you on, make you want something you didn't want and then make you wait and maybe not come across after all. Looking as bored as she could without falling over something, she shook hands and left, hoping she had left an impression of availability rather than desperation.

Out on the sidewalk she was suddenly, ravenously hungry. It was just a little after ten but the strain of the interview had left her nerves raw. Her shoes hurt. Her belt was too tight. Her hat pressed heavily on her sinuses. All the pressure points screamed for release.

This job would be the answer. Complete autonomy. Security, an outlet for her energies. Financial independence. And best of all, an immediate answer to her homelessness.

Groupsville would have to close ranks around her. She would become a traveling member, popping into town at intervals with hilarious stories about provincial women—and perhaps provincial men.

Hunger slowed her to a standstill before a drugstore. She had not eaten breakfast because interviews usually gave her cramps unless she had an empty stomach. There was only forty cents in her bag. No breakfast. No taxi either.

Taking the bus home, she flung off her clothes once inside the door and rushed to the kitchen. Wrapped in aluminum foil behind a bottle of lemon juice was the cold steak she had acquired from dinner with Martin, forgotten until this moment. She had forgotten Martin's other gift, too. It must still be in the evening bag she had thrown carelessly into some corner upstairs. The job had come not a moment too soon. She must be in a bad way to forget about money. It would have been fun ordering the ninety cent breakfast special in that restaurant and paying for it with a hundred dollar bill.

"That's the smallest I have," she would have said. But not "Keep the change."

Steak in hand, she galloped upstairs. The meat tasted okay. She idly hoped food poisoning wasn't activated by aluminum foil as she searched for the bag, finding it on the floor under her bed. The money was there, of course.

An ecstasy of acquisitiveness shook her. She would hoard every red cent until she had at least three thousand dollars American as a stake. Then off to Europe with the new wardrobe. Three thousand could last an awfully long time particularly if you didn't count on paying for meals and accepted transportation as it came along. In Europe, someone was always going somewhere and wanted company. She could live on Max's allowance easily and use the three thou for special

156

projects. This time she would not be afraid to travel where and how she pleased. The last time, she had hooked up with Kipcik and carried his camera bag, a humble follower. Next time, let everyone else watch out for her dust!

The red meat restored her energy. She dialled the answering service. Ingrid had already called and would think she'd been out all night. That was the trouble with early appointments. Nobody believed you.

"Ingrid . . . hi! It's not even eleven and I've been up and out for hours. And I may have a really spectacular job!"

"How marvellous!" Ingrid enthused with more than her usual gusto. "But my news is even more exciting. Ready? I'm getting married!"

"Great! To Philip?"

"No!" Ingrid said with a shade of annoyance. "To Bernard, of course!"

"Of course!" she exclaimed with a pang of self-pity. "I'm so happy for you! When? Where?"

"Thursday. At City Hall. And you're my best man. You have to stand up for me, Missy."

Thursday was Eviction Day, too. "That'll show Bernard's mother—and Philip Winston!"

"It was Philip who did it! Bernard was so jealous he couldn't stand it. We're going to Haiti and then Caracas. But don't think I've forgotten about you. When the big bad men make you move out you're coming right here. It works out perfectly. You move in here Thursday and when we get back I'll move in with Bernard and we'll figure it out from there. Musical apartments. See what a friend I am? Getting married just so you'll have a place to live. Damned nice of me, if I say so myself."

"I'll always remember your sacrifice," Melissa intoned. "But Ingrid, seriously, do you really want to marry Bernard? It's revolting of me to remind you, but I hate to see you making a mistake even though it means I get a jazzy place to live."

All effervescence gone, Ingrid said, "I'm being practical. How much longer can I compete?"

She didn't wait for an answer but quickly changed the subject. "We're going to elope and THEN tell the Nahoums. Oh, Missy, after all this time I think I've made the right decision! There's nothing more pathetic than an aging cover girl. Remember when I met you and that crazy Don Kipcik in Paris?"

Melissa remembered and suddenly, the Paris grass shone a nostalgic green.

"Well, lately I've been thinking about Francoise Baudette, the French girl I was rooming with. Tall—cadaverous—about 32, a seasoned vet! All the girls went to her for advice. Well, about a month after you and the Kipper disappeared into the Dolomites, Francoise disappeared, too. She didn't come home for three nights," Ingrid recalled. "Nobody thought much about it—we didn't exactly keep a bed check on each other. And then they found her floating in the Seine. The work had stopped. The bills were piling up and the boy she was in love with left her for someone else. I've never forgotten her scrapbook. Magazine covers, newspaper clippings, fancy brochures—all showing a beautiful girl in out-of-date clothes. That's not going to happen to me! Gotta run now and buy me an authentic Caribbean type trousseau. Check you later."

Mrs. Bernard Nahoum presiding at Charity Tea for Juvenile Delinquents . . . Mrs. Bernard Nahoum named America's Best-Dressed Society Woman . . . Mrs. Bernard Nahoum gives an intimate party aboard the yacht, *Ingrid*, named for her by her husband, the prominent banker.

Mrs. Bernard Nahoum was going to have a ball!

Driving down the East River Drive to meet Bernard at his office, Ingrid loosened her hair and allowed the wind to whip it straight back like an Egyptian frieze. She roared past the United Nations building, the new and old Bellevue Hospitals, the red brick housing projects that loomed prison-like above the squalor. As Manhattan Island narrowed to the point on the great harbor where East and Hudson Rivers converge, warehouses and produce markets hugged the shore.

At the Wall Street turn-off, Ingrid veered sharply, decelerated and lost control of the wheel.

The shiny red car spun on its axis in a wild pirouette and slammed against the retaining wall. It bounced back into the lane, facing in the right direction, Ingrid's hands frozen to the wheel, her blonde hair a tangled mat over her terrified eyes.

A motorcycle cop waved away the few curious motorists.

''Young lady, by rights you should be dead. I've been trying to catch you for half a mile. You were going eighty-five miles an hour!''

Movement returned. She pushed back her hair and automatically pulled a hairbrush from her capacious handbag to repair the damage. ''My God!'' was all she could say. ''The car got away from me. My God!''

''If anything had been in your way, I'd be wiping

up the mess right this minute. This is your lucky day, lady."

She laughed nervously. "Yes, officer, It is my lucky day. I'm on my way to City Hall for a marriage license . . ." Shock had not shattered her instinctive guile.

"If I were your boy friend, I would give you a good spanking."

"When he sees this car he'll do more than that!"

The policeman examined the side of the car. "You're luckier than I thought. Hardly dented. He won't notice it if you don't tell him."

"He'll never let me drive again . . ." she wailed in a heartbreaking cry to tear the hearts of monsters. Cunning now replaced guile. She must shake this cop. Bernard would be waiting. She didn't want him angry during these delicate few days.

"You've been very kind, officer," she said. "I'm okay now. May I go on? He's waiting." She pretended not to know about such vulgarities as traffic tickets.

"Well . . ." he was wilting ". . . I should give you a ticket but from the look on your face I don't think you'll drive that fast again. So I'll let you off as a wedding present. Now don't let me catch you on a slab in the morgue or you'll destroy me faith in people." He grinned a wide Irish grin and sped away.

"Thank you . . ." she called after him.

It was not the day to be killed. She had worked too hard to be laid out without a wedding ring on her hand.

Bernard crossed the sidewalk as she pulled up. "Hi, darling. Be careful. You're stopping traffic," he said with obvious pride.

She knew full well the stir created by a beautiful

160

blonde in a red sports car coming to collect a tall, slim sensitive looking young man who had the mark of wealth stamped on his high, narrow forehead, horn-rimmed glasses, hawk-like nose and straight white teeth that were a triumph or orthodontia.

The financial community is a small one. Bernard's sallow complexion colored as he played his part in the romantic vignette for the benefit of passers-by, many of whom knew him by sight.

An exquisite blonde who loved him. An expensive foreign car. Both in the name of Bernard Nahoum. He liked the whole idea. Having made the decision he now wondered why it had taken him so long to see the light. It was like that with every important decision. You fiddled and rationalized and examined and backed away for an objective view. But once decided, the simplicity of it all was astounding.

That was what made leaders of industry.

Decision.

Not the right decision or the wrong decision. But any decision that created a forward motion. Most problems could be solved in a hundred ways but everyone was always waiting for one person to say, "Here's how we do it. Follow me."

"I've never seen you so radiantly beautiful," he said, kissing her upturned face.

She slid over to give him the driver's seat. After all, it was his car. Also, her hands were a bit shaky.

"Where to?"

"Straight to the sun," she commanded.

"Dedalus at the controls!"

She had no idea what he was talking about but smiled.

"I should blindfold you," he said, leading her through a wide granite doorway. "This is a very secret route to the sun."

They ascended in the special Club elevator and emerged into a red plush hush lined with mahogany panels.

"This is the last bastion of masculinity," he said. "Here you can see the ghosts of the Morgans and Fisks and Goulds and hear old men talking about the good old days before the war, knowing they mean 1917."

Ingrid wished she could cover her hair. It was too bright. "But I don't see any lady bankers."

"No, and you won't. Not in there, anyway. We have to go around the corner to the Ladies Dining Room."

This newer section of the club was decorated in drab pastels and faded chintzes, a last-ditch sniping at the incursion of women. No plush here. Double doors opened out into a flagstone terrace where tables and chairs were set up amongst potted plants of indeterminate species.

"I think we can snag the last table in the sunshine," Bernard said with boyish eagerness. "Now—is this close enough to the sun for you?"

New York harbor lay spread out far below, a shimmering blue enamel softened by a fine noon haze. Ribbons of Brooklyn traffic hugged the shoreline to the left, hundreds of ships crawling to and from the open sea in well-ordered lines, the Statue of Liberty's crown shooting off sparks of reflected sunlight and in the distance, a little to the right, Staten Island, squatting large and low on the horizon like a giant mud

162

turtle. Over it all wafted the sharp salt air floating in from beyond the Ambrose Lightship.

Ingrid closed her eyes and inhaled deeply. She would be happy with this man. He had given her the sun when she asked for it.

"You look like a Viking Queen with your profile against the sky," Bernard whispered, groping for her hand. (She had not told him about her Italian ancestry. If their children were dark, she would blame it on his side of the family.)

"I've got the tickets," he said. "We'll go for the license after lunch and I've arranged for the father of a friend of mine to marry us Thursday afternoon. He's a judge. Then I go quietly back to work with a foolish grin on my face and pick you up at six-thirty. I've said I'm taking a few weeks off to go sailing. A bottle of champagne will be waiting for us at Idlewild to get us through the business of customs and then dinner on the plane and arrival in Haiti by moonlight."

"You guarantee the moonlight?"

"I most assuredly guarantee the moonlight, if I have to pay someone to stand outside the window with an electric light bulb."

"Oh, Bernard. We *are* going to be happy."

The Club steward cleared his throat. "Begging your pardon, Mr. Nahoum. There's a telephone call for you in the lounge."

"Excuse me, darling. Hope I haven't lost all our money just because I couldn't resist having lunch with a beautiful woman."

He returned moments later, his face haggard his cheekbones looked as if they might break through the translucent skin.

"What happened! Did you lose everything? It's all right, darling. We can go to Coney Island for our honeymoon."

"No—nothing like that." He swallowed the remainder of his martini. "It was—the *other* Mrs. Nahoum." He tried to make a joke of it. "She was just finishing up some business down here and wanted to join me if I were lunching alone. She knows I usually come here."

"Is she coming?" Ingrid asked softly. "I can manage it, darling."

"No—" He patted her hand but the reassurance was for himself. "I told her I was having an important lunch . . . a very important lunch . . . I love you very much, Ingrid."

"I love you, too, Bernard," she said. "But let's be gay. The vichysoisse will get warm if we don't eat it. Even your mother can't ruin my appetite."

"There's one thing," he ventured.

"What?" she demanded sharply. "That we're not getting married or something minor like that?" The near-accident had made her jumpier than she thought.

"No . . . no! Darling! Nothing like that. Please don't. It's just that I told her I'd come to dinner tomorrow night. I'm not going to be there Friday, of course. In fact she'll have our cable for her dinner Friday so I think I should be with her tomorrow night."

"What do I do? Have dinner with Philip?"

"Ingrid . . ." For a terrible moment, she thought he was going to cry. "Ingrid . . . that isn't worthy of you. I know I've procrastinated. I know these few days are going to be nerve-wracking for both of us.

164

I know we should have been married for months by now. Please be a little bit more patient with me."

She was contrite. "I'm sorry, Bernard. You're finding out what a bitch I am. Of course I understand. I'll be busy tomorrow night anyway doing all those little things brides are supposed to do, and you can come for a nightcap, darling."

She took both his hands. The soup got warm and the steward took it away. She had finished most of hers.

Returning uptown by the same route she kept her eye on the speedometer. Next time she'd be mashed to a pulp. Swedish beauty turned into smorgasbord in crack-up. Then wouldn't Philip be sorry? Probably for about ten minutes.

Bernard was her answer, the life force on whom she would revolve. If they ever had a daughter she would see to it that she had more than one rich young man to choose from.

The fresh air, the wine at lunch, the steady hum of tires lulled her into a oneness with the machine beneath her. A lady centaur if there was such a thing with a Viking figurehead and a vermillion body of not one horse but 220.

In a trance, she passed the 42nd Street turn-off which led from the highway to her apartment, as well as the next and the next. At 110th Street where the signs pointed to Queens and the Bronx, she suddenly knew where she was going.

It had been two years since she'd seen her mother and that was on her return from Europe after a three-year absence. She sent money home every week and telephoned occasionally. Her mother had not been out of the Bronx for maybe thirty years. Ingrid excused her own neglect with the complaint that it was more complicated getting to the Bronx than flying cross-country.

Her mother would be home, she was sure. If not helping out in the store, she would be sitting on a folding chair in front of the door. They had a telephone in the apartment now, but Momma was afraid of it. To her it meant bad news. Telegrams were worse. When Ingrid flew to Paris the first time she had cabled news of her safe arrival because all the other passengers were doing it and because for a lonely moment she wanted some contact with her kin.

She learned later her mother had screamed at the sight of the cable, scaring the delivery boy. She would not allow her husband to open the envelope. Not knowing about death prevented it from happening.

The whole family was uncomfortable with her now. Her success intimidated them. They took her money but talked behind her back. The choice had been hers and she was glad she had made it. Whenever she had doubts one recollection brought her back to reality. The summer vacation she had spent helping out in the store, sorting vegetables, staining her hands with berries, soaking her feet at night after standing all day.

The Bible says each generation must plan for the next. She didn't judge her family for not providing for her happiness. They had done their best and like all Italian children she naturally assumed her duty of sending them money.

*Her* children would never have to do that. They would profit from the culture and wealth of their father and the down-to-earth reality of their mother. They

166

would inherit the earth. They would be able to afford being meek.

Driving through the run-down neighborhoods, she was sorry she had taken the sports car. It was too ostentatious. A taxi would have been better. She hoped her mother would be glad to see her. While she was not going to reveal her wedding plans, some primitive instinct made her yearn for her mother's blessing.

Before too long she would tell Bernard about herself and bring him up to meet her family. For a reason she could not understand, she had told Philip, perhaps as a challenge. According to Fairy Tales, men were supposed to fall in love with you despite your background but Philip had missed his cue. Intuition prevented her telling Bernard. The Golden Girl illusion must not be spoiled by the aroma of meat balls and spaghetti.

As she pulled into a parking space in front of the store, a battery of small boys swarmed over the car.

"Hey, lady . . ." one said, in a coarse nasality that she had forgotten, "Wha's ziss? A Rolls Royce or sumpin'?"

"Shaddup, you jerk! It's a Mercedes. A German car. Don't you know nuthin'?"

"Yeah?"

"Yeah!"

A small, slim figure in a black dress and neat oxfords stood in the doorway of the store, her back to the street, a large watering can suspended over a box of finocchio.

"Momma," Ingrid whispered, stopping a few feet away.

The figure continued sweeping the array of vegetables with criss-crossing arcs of water.

Had she seen?

Was she deliberately turning her back?

"Momma? It's me . . ."

The woman turned. Two years had not aged her. The tight smooth skin and pale blue eyes were those of a girl, untouched by cosmetics. Her white hair was combed back into a silken knot, her delicate ear lobes pierced with small gold rings worn thin by the years. Her grandmother had eased them through her tender skin before she could walk. Except for a wedding band, they were her only ornament.

"Anna," she said stiffly. "You are in trouble?"

"No, Momma—I just came to see you. I wanted to see you. And Poppa. Where is he? He's all right?"

"Yes. He is delivering. The boy is sick. Poppa had to ride the bicycle. A good customer ordered some of the hot house fruits we keep in the big refrigerator. We are grateful to you for buying the refrigerator. It helps in the competition with the supermarket."

She spoke formally as if at a funeral.

Ingrid wanted to be swept into the warm embrace she knew was in the rigidly held arms. "What are you talking about? Grateful? I'm your daughter. It's my pleasure and privilege to help you and make your life easier. It's only right for a child to do these things for parents."

"It is right when the parents have satisfied the child. We have not satisfied you, Anna. You have become a new person, not Anna, not part of us. You owe us nothing."

Ingrid wanted to shake her, to pick up the frail black doll with the bones as exquisitely small as her own and shake her hard. Momma wanted her own way.

168

You weren't permitted to leave home. If you did, you were lost forever. They took the money all right. That did not offend them.

If Ingrid had sat on the front doorstep and married the local butcher maybe they would have combined stores into a family market by now. That would have made her the family saint!

All at once she felt like the American tourists she had seen while posing for a fashion layout in a rural area of Ireland. The tourists had come to see their fathers' birthplace, to meet family they'd never known, bringing stories and goodies from fabled America. She remembered one particular group who drove up to a small cottage in a large rented car. They tumbled out, self-consciously loaded down with cameras and gifts for the family clustered in the doorway like a Sara Algood tragedy.

That night, when the visitors had left, she and her party were having a pint at the local when the faces seen earlier in the doorway arrived en masse and ordered a round of stout. Their picturesque quality faded away as they mimicked their benefactors and reconstructed the great act they had put on to earn a few dollars.

"I want your life to be easier, Momma. America has given me a good income . . ."

"For showing yourself? For letting men take your picture? For parading yourself before them and letting them think things about your body? You are not the orphan of Napoli like these Sophia Lorens and Lollobrigidas. The money is sinful and we are sinful for spending it. May God forgive us."

"I've earned the money. There is no reason to be

169

ashamed. And soon, if all goes well, I'm going to buy you a house, right in this neighborhood if you want it. Poppa can sell the store and I'll help him invest the money so there's an income. Then you can both take a trip back to Italy made. . . ."

"We're happy the way we are, Anna. If you have so much money, give it to St. Francis. The building fund is having a drive."

(A customer asked for one tomato and two large onions. Seventeen cents.)

"Can I do something while I'm waiting for Poppa?"

"There's nothing to do."

She picked up a watering can.

"These grapes look dry. Maybe I can . . ."

It was wrenched from her hand.

"That is my job. You do not belong here. You can not come and expect to help. Once in two years is not enough for fruit and vegetables."

Ingrid stared at the kaleidoscope of fruits and vegetables with a fusion of wild despair and deep loathing. The pavement beneath her feet was chipped and spattered with chewing gum blobs and half-erased potsies. Garbage hugged the curb and in places splashed across the gutter into the path of cars.

A gang of teen-age boys in blue jeans and identical jackets jostled past her, their long hair oiled back in the duck's ass style, their faces erupted from the irritation of premature shaving.

One of them turned a few feet away and whistled through his teeth.

"Some babe. Some bambina. Hey, blondie. How about a quick one, hah? A real quick one? Hnnnnnnh?"

170

He made an obscene gesture with one hand halfway up the other arm.

Ingrid stared with disgust as her mother rushed at them with her watering can.

One more minute and Ingrid would scream.

"Get away from her, you stinking brats," she snarled at three little children sitting on the fender. They scurried off. She bruised her hip in her haste to get into the car and away.

"Tell Poppa I couldn't wait!" she said. She knew her mother was right there but she did not look up, giving her attention to the car and the traffic and getting away as fast as possible.

Let them work till they dropped if that's what they wanted! She was getting married on Thursday!

Melissa prowled, wondering what to do with herself. The idle poor. Everything she might want to do cost money. There was always the library but that meant leaving the phone.

The service would pick up calls, she reminded herself.

Well, the library was too dim, too far, too airless.

She must get Ingrid a wedding gift. It could wait until she returned from the Caribbean. Wedding gifts were not like birthday gifts. You didn't have to give them on the exact day. She would wait for Ingrid's color scheme. Black and blue was what she had jokingly told her own friends, which Max had not found funny.

She stretched out on her bed. If one appointment was so exhausting, how could she handle a job? Assuming she *got* the job. Bill Butler had seemed impressed. She could feel it when men were impressed. Her only problem was when a man was attracted to her she wanted to prove to him that his instincts were right.

The afternoon papers would be out by now. Going all the way to the corner for them was too much trouble.

The phone rang. Her juices promptly began to flow.

Bill Butler offering her twice the money?

Old Coochie with a new elephant?

"Your picture's in the afternoon paper. You look great, just bored enough."

It was Walter.

"Oh, really?" she asked, trying to sound just bored enough. "Must be that committee jazz. I think I'll ask them to forget grandma and make me their next project."

"Things couldn't be that bad, not for a pretty girl like you."

Molasses made her gag. She kept silent.

"Look, Melissa . . . I know I'm the person you can most likely live without but . . . well, if you're not too busy, I'd be grateful if I could come over and do some fancy measuring."

There were worse ways to kill an afternoon. Groupsville was not foregathering until six.

"Okay, if you'll bring me the afternoon papers." (Always get them to bring something.)

She slid back into her dress and was running a brush through her hair when he leaned on the doorbell.

"Where were you? At the corner?"

"How'd you guess? Here are your papers, lady. *Sa-*

172

*a-a-ay!* That's quite a dress. You look efficient and sexy at the same time.''

"You should see it with the hat. Sheer intimidation. It's my conning outfit. I wore it this morning to con a man into giving me a job.''

"Did he con easily?''

"I'm not sure. The dress has been cleaned. Its con power may have worn off. All those strong chemicals.''

"I getcha. It's like rain-proofing. But don't know about wearing off. I feel myself inexplicably drawn to you.''

Did he think she had forgotten their tender little scene of Saturday night and his petulant exit line?

When confused, attack!

"Where's your T-Square, Mr. Architect? Don't you carry it with you at all times? A three-pronged phallic symbol, wouldn't you say, you being the expert on symbols? Architecture is *soo* masculine, it sends shivers up by backbone, Walt. There is one thing I've been dying to know, one thing I've hesitated to ask you.''

"What's that?'' he asked, on guard.

"Do you suffer from an edifice complex?''

He smiled. Then he laughed.

"I hope you didn't pull that on the boy who interviewed you today. The reason everyone hates puns is that they didn't think of them first.''

"I happen to like puns!'' She closed her eyes defiantly. The sunlight danced on the splash of blue eye shadow coating her upper lids.

It dazzled him. He was a man who read the ads and at least glanced at the fashion section while turning

173

to the sports page. From his recent months in the field, as it were, he could recognize the tricks. The artifice. The wily deceptions that jarred the hunter instinct. Recognizing the hoax didn't lessen the effect.

Take the little red-haired project, for instance. Watching her get ready was better than a floor show. A thing around the waist to pull it in. A thing around the chest to push it up. A layer of goo on the face that made her look dead while gradually she added a dot of red, a smear of white, a dollop of blue. Brushed, pencilled, mashed into submission.

It was a little like watching a master chef ice a beautiful cake. Every additional flurry made your heart sing more while all you could think about was getting your teeth into it.

"You have a point," he conceded.

She could tell his pendulum was swinging in her direction. A field expert herself, she could read his thoughts which were as old fashioned as grandfather's clock.

It was two o'clock. Bullfighters dreaded five o'clock. *At five in the afternoon* . . . In New York City, something happened to men at two in the afternoon, which, when you came to think of it, was five in the afternoon in Spain, give or take a time zone.

At two in the afternoon . . . usually over coffee and brandy in a quiet restaurant . . . something happened to men. They began to think of driving to the sea or sitting in the darkened balcony of Radio City Music Hall or taking a nap somewhere.

Walter was getting that look.

"I shall substitute poetry for punnery. 'Mad is the heart of love and gold the gleam of his wing . . .' "

"Oh, no!"

Poetry-spouters were the worst. How can you interrupt Shelley or turn down Shakespeare? There was only one way to handle this.

"Who are you quoting? Edgar Guest?"

It worked. He sat down and lit a cigarette. "Hippolytus is not someone you can joke about."

"You take whatever you like seriously. I'll have my little jokes, if you don't mind."

He stood up. "Your whole life is a joke. Everything strictly for laughs. A revolving door into the fun house. Well, what time do the doors open?"

He stood up as close as he could without touching her, conscious of the bits of tobacco stabbing his tongue and the grain of her skin inches away.

She held her breath. Men made her feel many different things. Cloister saint or Pushover Polly, she could usually manage a flavor of romance.

Not this time! Walter made her feel cheap. Shabby. Degenerate. Not that he wanted to reform her like a good hero. He was more the vice officer who closed down the house after he collected the evidence personally.

It takes one to know one. Perverts recognize each other. By now, men must instantaneously recognize her for what she was, what she had become, what she would stop being as of next Monday. *If* she got the job. The cure. The 25-City sanitarium with hundreds of women as therapy.

She swayed against him. It was impossible for her to resist a man who wanted her. Max had said he wanted her but couldn't prove it. All the others had proved to her again and again how much she was wanted.

It's a shock to suddenly realize you're an addict. That you're standing on the brink of another binge and there's nothing you can do to stop yourself.

The phone thrust them guiltily apart.

She ran to it.

Reprieve. Someone named Vera Haggerty was saying that Ingrid had suggested her as a last-minute replacement as Mistress-of-Ceremonies for a fashion show at the Waldorf at four. The girl who was doing it had been rushed to the hospital with bursting appendix. Could she come right over?

Could she? Like a hot! Bless Ingrid. Bless Vera Haggerty. Bless all those women on their way to the Waldorf in hats that were too small and furs that were too big.

"Must run," she said. "You can stay and measure anything you like. Just slam the door on your way out. Oh—and if you get hungry—" she paused dramatically "—there's a jar of peanut butter in the kitchen."

She could feel her cheeks flushed and excited. She knew her eyes were shining. Men were a valuable cosmetic. She had begun the cure. Instead of a complete break, she would cut herself down to a small shot of titilation in the early afternoon, but no chaser!

It was going to be a good day after all. A few dollars coming in from the fashion world. Groupsville was meeting for drinks at Michael's Pub. Maybe, in the meantime Bill Butler would have called to give her the job, which now she wanted more than anything in the world.

"Melissa . . ." It was a different Walter stopping

her at the door. A woman's having somewhere else to go changed a man's attitude.

"I'm probably wrong to leave you here. I'm liable to come back and find my things on the sidewalk."

"Melissa, shut up. What I've been trying to do since I got here is apologize for being a shit Saturday night. That's all. One bastard reporting in. You never gave me a chance. Is it me or do you act like this with all men?"

"I'm afraid I haven't time for a dissertation on the subject. Summed up in a few words, I have found that if I treat a man like a man, he shrinks at the responsibility and dives for the door. If I put my finger in his eyes and then make him apologize for having his eye in my way, he thinks I'm quite a gal. Work it out with your T-Square. Me for the Waldorf and the treachery of fashion."

"One more question. Answer me honestly, Melissa. What do you want in a man?"

He was trying to find out where he had failed. His wife. Himself. The women who came and went with their little makeup cases.

She signalled a taxi to stop and wait. Leaning on one elbow against the open door, she said, "I want him to be everything. Lover. Brother. Husband. Doctor. Seducer. Anything but son . . . the taxi is waiting."

He watched the cab pull away and closed the door. Other people's homes seemed different when you were there alone. He dialled a phone number.

"Dana? Walter. Yes . . . I know we haven't been very friendly lately. I'm calling to say I've changed my mind. You can have the divorce. Can we have lunch tomorrow to talk about it? Fine. One o'clock.''

Melissa had a big mouth but she had said a mouthful. The truth had come to him with the clarity of pain. As a married girl-chaser, exempt from commitments, absolutely free to come and go as he pleased, Walter Simpson was suddenly tired of coming and going, finally satiated by one too many pair of luscious lips, succulent breasts, juicy thighs, the plump young pigeons who were the same girl over and over again. Dana as she had been. Dana the night he first met her doing the Big Apple, wearing a swing skirt with boy's suspenders and a ridiculous bow-tie the girls affected, and filthy saddle shoes scrawled over with red nail-polish autographs.

Dana had been, quite literally, Queen of the Campus, with the kind of beauty that won contests. The natural, healthy good looks, the faceless face glorified in beer ads. the even-featured symmetry that was beautiful by default. Because there was no jarring prominence, no disproportion of line or contour, no glaring anomaly to prevent her being beautiful, she was therefore beautiful.

Now, more than twenty years later, he was still obsessed with possessing the campus queen. Dana had taken her loving cup on their honeymoon and now it lived in a glass case over the bar. Never a vain beauty, Dana had enjoyed the adulation, accepted the husband she'd won as Beauty Queen but had not understood, nor subsequently kept up, her end of the bargain which was to be eternally lovely.

What had never occurred to her was that after twenty-five, a woman's beauty is determined by two

178

distinct forces, the Inner and the Outer. From inside came humor, intellect, sexuality and the essentially feminine reactions to love, fear and curiosity. The external imprint was solely a matter of craftsmanship, perfection of female skills in the use of the body, cosmetics, colors and textures to create and intensify the continuing illusion of desirability.

Dana's feminine instincts had failed her, perhaps because she had never needed to develop them. When love and affection bordering on worship are yours from childhood, they become an accepted and expected part of the life scheme. When they are inexplicably withdrawn, the resulting helpless bewilderment only makes things worse.

Walter had not seen his wife in several months. The last time had ended with a pathetic scene, punctuated by a hysterical hangover, a drink-stained nightgown and the gray flaccidity of once firm flesh. Late another night, in the men's room at Toots Shor's, he had overheard two young men discuss her by name as an aging beauty who liked to lush it up in Third Avenue clip joints and could always be counted on to pick up the tab, except that a guy had to be very careful or she might take him home with her.

When Dana replaced the phone she knocked over the glass she had put down to answer it, splashing tomato juice on her skirt.

"Stand still, clumsy. Don't move. I'll mop it up in a second," said the short, stocky man whose hand had not left her waist during the conversation.

She stood unmoving, a statue of obedience.

"He makes me nervous, Fred. That's all."

179

"He's changed his mind, hasn't he? He's giving you the divorce?"

"Yes, but why?"

Fred brushed the red droplets off the gray wool dress.

"What difference why. He knows nothing of me. Give him the divorce and then we'll marry."

"Yes, Fred. You're right. What would have happened to me that night if you hadn't come into that bar?"

"We're going to forget everything that happened to you before that night, Mr. Walter Simpson included. Your life began with me."

She went to his arms, the first arms she had gone to sober in the months since Walt had left. He had scooped her out of the martini like a squashed, sodden olive. He had comforted her to sleep, awakened her to sunshine, sent her packing to the hairdresser. He was a man who knew what he wanted and wasn't afraid to ask a woman to give it to him. Dana was a warehouse brimming over with things to give him, things that no one had ever thought to ask of her.

Melissa was enjoying herself. It was exciting to have hundreds of people in rapt attention to your words, even if they were all women and the words weren't exactly yours.

Men could never understand the delirium of fashion, the turmoil in each mind as one after another the new silhouettes, colors and fabrics minced into the spotlight. This could be her turning point. For the first time, she was as one with a roomful of women—gasping, admiring, remembering a detail here, a line there, sharing with them the exultation of a purely female function.

Forgotten were husbands, bankbooks, men who drank all your liquor. Here, coming down the runway, were love and desire, greed and lust. To have this. To wear that. Each woman saw her own face above the swaying figures and imagined what would happen as a result.

The closest a man could get to this paradox of mass appreciation and individual craving was a burlesque show. The comparison stopped with the elements of music, spotlights, a runway and girls.

Men had their clubs. Women had their fashion shows. The first was a conspiracy against women, the second, a conspiracy toward men.

Melissa had Groupsville, too.

Before leaving the shambles of tissue paper, programs, half-eaten tea sandwiches and spilled face powder, Melissa checked her answering service.

Bill Butler had not called. How many others were waiting for his sincere voice to say, ''We've decided. You're it!''

She wanted desperately to be *It*. She was tired of home base and wanted to venture out. Even though it made her a target she wanted to be way out in front where everyone would have to take giant steps to catch her. By the rules of the game, she could always turn and catch them first.

It was six. She decided to be late for Groupsville. The earlier you arrived, the more you drank. Michael's gave you baby hot dogs and spicy shrimp to sharpen your thirst. It got to be a toss-up between getting sick

181

on too many hors d'oeuvres or the too many drinks needed to calm the troubled salivary glands.

Refreshed and re-painted, Melissa arrived at Michael's Pub. It was six-twenty-six.

"Hi, beautiful," the Maitre d' greeted her. "You having dinner with us tonight?"

"Nope. Just drinks. We can't afford to eat and drink, too! Let's be realistic, darling."

"Mr. Minto is at the corner table."

Halfway down the bar, an arm shot out and yanked her into a bruising clinch. The arm belonged to Don Kipcik. The bruises were the three cameras he wore inside his jacket.

"Well," she said. "I haven't destroyed myself in at least five minutes. I can't quite place the face but the smell is the same. When are you going to get a new raincoat?"

She'd have known that raincoat in the dark. It was an exaggeration of tabs and buttons covered with the accumulated grime of five continents and fifteen years of photographing everything from puberty rites in Brazil to street fighting in Beirut.

The coat was his talisman. He joked about it but he believed it. The Signal Corps had taught him to use a camera during the war. The first thing he bought afterwards was a camera. He happened to be Hartford the day of the circus disaster. From the sale of his pictures to a syndicate, he bought the raincoat.

A citizen of the world, a technical resident of Chicago where his parents had brought him as a child from Poland, Kip was an Anglophile. England's culture, its history, tradition and emotional restraint had captured him completely. He was absolutely convinced the raincoat made him look terribly British. He liked the name Kipper given him because of his passion for the British breakfast favorite.

"When the raincoat goes, I go. I want to be buried in it," he said. "You still have that very bad habit of saying something bad to me instead of something nice. Like how glad you are to see me after all these years."

"Why should I be glad?"

"Melissa. You cannot still be bitter? I told you when we started that photographers cannot be trusted."

"Well, at least that's something.'

"What is?"

"That you remember me at all. I did not appreciate waking up in the Hotel Rapido with twenty thousand lira pinned to the pillow."

"There was a bunch of mimosa, too. I am not insensitive. I had to go to Aswan to photograph the city that would be changed by a certain infamous dam. You could not go. It was very sad. I could not bear to tell you. A woman's tears I cannot stand. They are why I am married, as you know."

"Still?"

"Still. She lives in Paris with the boy."

"How old is he now?"

"Oh, I don't know. Seven. Eight."

He shrugged.

"You mean you don't know how old your own little boy is?"

"There you go. Sentimental. He is a very nice little boy. Dione has money. I send her more. He is cared for. I did not want a child. Nor a wife. Perhaps when he is grown, assuming I am still alive, we shall meet and introduce ourselves. But what of you? I heard

183

from the grapevine that you married? Is that your husband staring so disapprovingly? Let's give him something to be jealous about. It will make him appreciate you more.''

He kissed her.

''For heaven's sake. Cut it out, Kip. That is *not* my husband. I'm divorced.''

Was he the reason for everything? Had she come full circle in four and a half years after tearfully leaving the still-warm but empty bed and catching the first plane back to New York? Meeting Max on the plane and deciding soon afterward that he was more loving, more solid, more rewarding than carrying camera bags for the last of a vanishing breed of itinerant journalists?

Indisputably, he was a great photographer. Indisputably, too, he was a loner, with a death wish as strong as his perception. So clearly could he see the tragedy of life, raw and bleeding under its cloak of richly woven travesty, that he couldn't bring himself to participate. It would be too painful. He could only observe and immortalize what he saw on film.

When people, especially women, got close to him, he couldn't stand seeing their nakedness revealed in the harsh light of reality. His lenses could strip the veneer off film stars and prime ministers, rebel leaders and men who were about to die. His lenses were his eyes. They told the truth where other photographers merely took pictures.

He saw too much, knew too much, felt too much. Impatience spurred him on to more bizarre places, more escapades, more probing of human behavior. There was a joke around the picture magazines that the first manned missile to the moon would contain

Kipcik who would tell the assembled Moon People, "Bring your leader to me."

"Well, Bublichki," he was saying, breathing a mixture of Gaulois and garlic that was not unpleasant, "The big Picture Editor upstairs must be looking out for me. I thought of calling you but married ladies are not interested in the working press. But I have thought of you, stupid little goose. It is all your doing that when I returned from the Nile and found you gone, I drowned my sorrow in a bottle of very cheap wine and fell in with an evil companion who stole my back tooth."

"Your *what*?"

"Yes." He opened his mouth, pointing a nicotine stained finger inside as he spoke. "She must have been a dentist. The tooth was solid gold. Eight hundred dollars American. It was gone from its moorings, neatly removed. I didn't miss it until three days later."

"How ghoulish." But she was enslaved again by this sad, exciting man who needed a haircut, who always told stories like this about himself but never about saving lives in the Holland flood or hanging from a helicopter by an ankle strap for an aesthetic satisfaction.

"You were right to leave," he said. "I think I wanted you to pack up camp while I was gone. We were becoming permanent."

"Ten months isn't permanent."

"The way we were, three weeks was permanent. You knew it. I knew it."

She had met Kip at a party in London on the first lap of her month's vacation, two weeks paid, two weeks on her own. After the party they had walked along the Thames Embankment until dawn sent them scurrying from the light to her hotel room overlooking Green Park.

Two days later she had left with him to cover a political rally in France. Three weeks later she had cabled her resignation to her New York agency from the Swiss chalet near a spot where five tourists had been mysteriously murdered.

"It will come as no surprise to you that I am once again looking for an assistant," he said, his strong thin mouth curved downward in a sardonic smile, his raven eyes fixed imploring.

"You go through assistants faster than France goes through premiers. Where to do this time? Inside Inside?"

"No. I am going to recreate St. Exupery's flight to Arras over the Andes in a single engine plane."

"Where will your assistant ride? On one of the wings? I saw that in a movie once, with Spencer Tracy I think."

"There are two seats."

"Where does the pilot sit?"

"I am the pilot."

His idea of flying was like swimming. You learned by doing.

Dominic had sent for a telephone. She could see him feverishly dialling. She knew he was annoyed at her taking so long to say hello to someone. Insville hated and mistrusted outsville.

"Well, nice seeing you, Kip. Let's get together sometime." The casual brush.

"I want you to come with me, Melissa. Three weeks in Caracas, a helicopter to the headwaters of the Amazon. Festival in Rio. A rest at Sao Paolo and then over the Andes. Now that I see you again, you're the only one I can consider. Say Yes at once!'' he commanded, his long, fierce fingers pressing across her palm.

He meant it. He lived on the spur of the moment. If there wasn't time to pack a bag, he left without it. His belongings were scattered all over the world. If his underwear gave out and it was inconvenient to buy some, he went without underwear. He was careless about everything except his cameras and the raincoat. He loved good food but could get by on beans. He loved luxurious trappings but could sleep standing up.

Five years before, Melissa had said Yes At Once and gone with him, certain in the certainty of innocence that this was the man and this the life for which she had been made.

He was, in essence, her first lover, perhaps her only truly romantic lover, joyously free of repressions, doubts, taboos and the aggressive shame that she had come to believe inherent in male behavior. Kip was all extravagant things. Ardent. Possessive. Protective. Affectionate in public; affectionate in private. Lavish with the gifts of his mind, his soul and his person.

Traveling with Kip was sex and sightseeing at their best. Melissa wanted to keep going forever, trade in her return ticket. That Kip felt the same way, she was sure, and when she asked him when they were getting married, it was to her mind a simple matter of setting the date.

Kip's first reaction had been horror—not at the thought of marrying Melissa, but at her romantic innocence and raw vulnerability, tragedies of so many young American girls. As kindly as he could, he told her about his wife and skipped out for Africa before she awoke in a rage of desire.

She could feel the flames of that fiery rage in the hollows of her cheeks. Nothing much had changed in five years—with about ten million exceptions. He was still married to Dione. If Melissa picked up his camera bags again, it would be history repeating itself. Knucklehead Revisited.

"When can I let you know?" she asked, unable to turn away completely.

"I'm leaving next week," he said. "This week, I take care of unfinished business."

She could imagine. There were unmistakable teeth marks on one ear-lobe and an angry blue bruise on his neck.

The decision was not hers. It would all depend on Bill Butler. If he didn't come through with that job, she would have no choice.


Dominic pretended she had just arrived.

"I was beginning to worry about you, darling. Just rang your number. Some chap answered. Said to tell you Mr. Butler's office rang. No message."

Whyever was Walter answering the phone? No wonder her service had no messages! She was furious. Now she would have to stew until morning to find out what Mr. Butler had to say. Didn't Walt know better than to answer someone else's phone?

"Introduced himself as Simpson. Said to apologize to you for picking up the phone. Left your number with his office and was expecting a call."

"Oh . . ."

"He asked me the most peculiar question."

"Yes? What?" Her guard was up.

"He wanted to know if I was a member of Groupsville."

She threw back her head and laughed at his confusion. Most of Groupsville did not call it that among themselves.

"Where's old Cooch-Poona?"

"He and Daphne have pressed off for Barbadoes. He's a bit nervy. Needs heat."

"Daphne looks like a built-in heating pad to me."

"Who was that chap you were so shamelessly kissing at the bar?"

"Oh, nobody. Just some beat-up photographer."

"Why are you women so made for photographers? It is a disease. Give a man a camera and the girls go wild. What is it about photographers, Melissa? You must tell me. Do they take you into the darkroom with all those chemicals? Is that the fascination?"

"It's because they're loners and wanderers," she said, "and they go their own way alone. People are always moaning about wanting to feel needed but it's more exciting to be with someone who really doesn't need you. Then you kid yourself into thinking that you're the girl who's going to supply that need—but you can't. No one can."

"But why photographers? What's so special about clicking a camera?"

"Oh, some girls go for jazz musicians. Some like lifeguards or ball players. Others go for the beat painters. It's all a phase you go through until you establish a deep, mature relationship like the one you and I have, Dominic."

"Touché! Have a gin. I'm on my fourth."

Groupsville grouped. A nucleus of eight. Iris Chekenian just returned from the Mayan Peninsula with a pair of earrings that threatened to elongate her ears. David Montgomery whirling between drink dates with writers, actors and angels for a play he was hoping to produce. Shari Lucas leaving for Hollywood on the midnight for a bit part in a television series that would not even pay the fare. "It's worth it," she kept saying. "Someone will discover me if I have to discover them first."

Different faces. Same old talk. Same old dreams and no serene resting place to dream them. She crossed her fingers and tried to cross her toes inside her shoes. By next Monday she would be out of this.

Kip left with an airy wave in her direction and a pantomimed, "Call me. I want you."

By ten o'clock the strain had begun to tell on her. It had been a long day. How often was she out by nine a.m.? Then Ingrid's news. The dance exercise class with Walt, the fashion show and to top it all, the Kipper. Most people threw away leftovers. She seemed to have a morbid predilection for stashing them away and dragging them out years later. Modern refrigeration was a snare and delusion.

"Me for beddie-byes," she stifled a yawn for Dominic's benefit. They had by this time reconvened at 21 where everyone was eating and wondering who was going to pay.

"I'll take you home."

"No, it's all right, Dominic. I don't want to cut into your evening. I'm bushed and I have an early appointment tomorrow."

190

To call Bill Butler first thing.

"I insist," he said.

They stood to go.

"Melissa's tired. I'm taking her home. Whoever pays, let me know how much I owe," he dismissed the financial problem.

"Thank you for running me home," she said a few minutes later at her doorstep. "I'm afraid I can't ask you in. I'm going to put my hair in pins and things like that. Destroy the illusion."

"Don't be a clot. Of course I'm coming in. I like to watch girls put their hair into pins."

He would not be diverted so she marched upstairs. *I won't even offer him a drink.*

Moments later he followed with a tinkling drink in each hand. He knew his way around the little house.

Seated at the dressing table in her slip with a plastic protector around her shoulders to catch the setting lotion, she set to work. Dominic sat in the doorway, watching intently.

"Tell me more about the man in the raincoat. What's his name?"

"Kip. Short for Kipper because he likes them. Short for Kipcik."

"A Polish Anglophile. We can use all comers. Since you have a weakness for adventure, did you know that I was a racing driver? I turned over in an Aston-Martin in the Grand Prix and stared at a hospital ceiling for six months."

"Oh, Dominic. How awful."

"If you can take your hands away from your own head and feel the back of mine you may detect a certain hardness that is not my British character but an aluminium plate."

"You told me you got that in the war when you were shot down in France."

"Well, it was both, really. When I got back they gave me a steel disc. You could break a finger on it. Damned uncivil. They warned me not to race but while your chaps were dreaming of white Christmases and all that, I was dreaming about the racer. Driving it through France you might say was my reason for fighting."

"Not for King and country?" she said with a mouthful of bobbie pins.

"*Queen* the country," he said with belligerence. There were tears in his eyes. Drink and patriotism do that to an Englishman.

"What do Americans know about patriotism? About love of country? About history and tradition and heritage. Britain is Mother England and America is the hideous, greedy child who destroys everything given to it and the parent as well. Suez was the death blow. Suez was the nasty halfwit putting arsenic in the tea instead of sugar. England is old and needed the physical strength of a young nation. Suez was a mistake from which we shall never recover. All we're good for now is folk festivals with morris dancers and pancake races. We've become a bloody side-show. Come to Old England where time stopped four hundred years ago. Poor Elizabeth. This one married her Philip. The other was courageous enough to tease her Philip and all the others for the good of the crown. Her Majesty is a tourist attraction for the grubby Texans and Wogs to peer at through their sunglasses and take photographs.''

He leaned his head against the door, closed his eyes and sighed deeply, spilling some of his drink.

"Dominic," she said, at a loss. What *could* she say? "Can't you try to be a little hopeful? Everyone's working desperately for peace. This country has made mistakes. So has yours. You have a good job. You have to work for your own success."

"On the telly? With scruffy Mums in carpet slippers eating their sausages and chips and expecting me to amuse them? Television has killed the films. We can thank America for that, too. British telly had a high standard of programming until America sent us the situation comedies!"

"If the British audiences didn't like them, they would have been sent back, but fast."

"You have the mistaken idea that people know what is to their best interest. It's a myth of democracy. Man wants to roll in the mud and eat whatever is easiest and makes no demands on his taste buds. Corn flakes. White bread. Frozen anything. Tasteless. Pointless. Easy. Nobody tell us anything is delicious. Only that it is *easy* and we must worship it. Man does not want to uplift himself. He wants to take the easy way and be praised for his discernment."

She tied a scarf around her head.

"I'm afraid it's curtain time, Dominic," she said kindly. She hadn't realized how drunk he'd become. "You really must go."

"Let me look at you with your head bandaged like a southern mammy. What happened to those delicious southern mammies that one sees in all Civil War films?

193

Are they all running for Congress? To be a woman and a Negro in the country must be dreadful. All the problems of men plus the racial issue. I worship you, white mammy.''

''Please, Dominic. I'm tired. Remember, I didn't invite you to stay. You insisted.''

''Yes. I like to see a beautiful creature being ugly in the pursuit of beauty. It's like watching the Creation, the molding of clay into an enchantress.''

''This enchantress is a pincushion of bobbie pins. Be an angel and leave.''

''Without beauty a woman is dead. I have made women beautiful, Melissa. My own wife included. She was a plain little thing when I married her and now she's an acknowledged beauty.''

She smiled. No more beauty from a jar. Beauty from a man, instead.

He rose and leaned heavily against the dressing table knocking over a bottle.

''You're a revolting baggage with your head bandaged that way.''

Now she was angry. Her reflection said he was right.

''Well, get the hell out of here, Dominic. I didn't ask you to sit in!''

He pulled her to her feet. ''Come, my ugly. Let me make you beautiful. I have an aluminium plate in my head and two false teeth in my mouth and my country has given herself to the Wogs, but there is still one thing I can do better than anyone in the world.''

He threw her to the bedroom floor. The plastic shoulder cover sliced into her neck, the pins dug into her head.

194

"Son of a bitch! You're messing up my hair!"

"I shall be inhumanly careful. Both you and your hair shall be radiant tomorrow for your appointment. The independent American spirit."

"If I were so independent, I would boot you down the stairs."

"Ah, my dear," he fell on top of her.

Executing a fast hip pivot, she rolled over and sprang to her feet. Catching him by his striped tie, she pulled him to the top of the stairs.

"Will you go? Or do I push?"

He lumbered down the steps and out the door without a word or a backward glance.

She slathered a cream masque on her face and left an eight o'clock call with her service. The training for normalcy had begun.

No sooner was she asleep than the phone exploded in her ear.

Dominic! She would have him deported. Well, she just wouldn't answer. Let the service take it. She heard the clicking sound that indicated Service had picked up. Gingerly she raised the receiver to listen . . .

"Oh, hello Mother. Sorry I took so long to answer. I was in the tub. Isn't this late for you to call?"

"Yes, but I know how late you stay up. We were visiting and we just got back and I haven't had a chance to call you. I spoke to Ellis just as we were leaving tonight and she told me about the eviction and . . ."

Melissa sank back in the pillows, the receiver propped up several inches from her ear. At that distance, her mother's voice sounded like a tape played backwards or a record on the wrong speed. Why hadn't Ellis kept her mouth shut? Yack, yack, yack. It was a new kind of breathing that the Navy might find useful for atomic submarines or frogmen. You just kept talking without a single pause for breath.

When the voice finally stopped, Melissa said, "Yes mother. I didn't want to worry you. I'm very tired. I'll call you tomorrow."

She hung up.

Rally round the loser. Have one bit of bad luck and everyone came to commiserate. Fall on your face and they formed a protective circle so you could lie in the mud in peace. No one would help you get up. Have a real tragedy and the world beat a path to your door.

She lay in the darkness rigid with fatigue and worry. The pins scratched her scalp. The bandana smothered her brain. The air in the room clogged her lungs. It was only ten after twelve. Eight hours to go. Leave it to Mom to call the first night in months that she went to bed early.

She fell asleep, finally, and dreamed of the women at the fashion show. They all began to chase her and as she ran, looking back, they all had Claire's face. She was running as fast as she could but it wasn't fast enough. They were gaining.

She was held back by a heavy weight in her arms. Babies. Hundreds of blue-bundled babies all with the faces of men she had known, fighting and clawing to be suckled by her. She closed her eyes tight, refusing to see their faces. She must not see their faces. No . . . No . . . *NO* . . .

The grate loomed ahead as she raced down the pavement. She fell to her knees, pulling at it, shaking it with all her might.

*"Let me in! Let me in!"*

# TUESDAY

In Greek mythology, *Momus* was an evil spirit, exiled from Olympus for nagging and mockery, proof that the Greeks not only had a word for it but a positive solution. Score another point for the classics.

Melissa had found this obscure classical fact at the dentist's. It was a filler at the end of an article on euthanasia that she was too jittery to read with the imminence of a drill on the other side of the door.

It was amazing what you could learn in a waiting room:

—Joseph Conrad's real name was Korzeniowski, although his middle name was Konrad with a K.

—Vichysoisse was invented in New York, not Paris.

—The Earl of Essex was only 18 when the 52-year-old Queen Elizabeth took a shine to him.

—Henry VIII owned 76 recorders.

(Melissa had taken recorder lessons at college as music correlation with English Lit. She had progressed to "Go Tell Aunt Rhody" when the boy she was pinned to had put the double whammy on the project.

A psychology major, he condemned the recorder as oral pacification and a substitute for thumb-sucking.

So how could she recognize the real thing when she couldn't recognize an obvious substitute?)

"Ring, damn you. Ring!" She yelled at the phone, concentrating on it with all her will. From supreme indifference the day before, she was now a quivering soufflé of enthusiasm about the job. She was frothy and delectable and hot out of the oven, ready and raring to go. Could not Bill Butler in his office sense that if she were not served up soon she faced deflation and the waste of expensive ingredients?

If she were smart, she would wait for Bill Butler to call her. Why did you always have to wait for a man to call you? It was maddening. By 9:58 she had smoked thirteen cigarettes. If he didn't call soon she might get lung cancer. In the interests of health, she called him.

As it turned out, Mr. Butler was in conference. He had asked his oily-larynxed secretary to apologize to Mrs. Kempton for not coming to the phone personally and to inform her that the decision on the job had been postponed for three weeks because of a policy complication. He (and his secretary) hoped Mrs. Kempton would understand.

Mrs. Kempton understood fine. Bill Butler was a coward. Like most men. Afraid of saying anything unpleasant to a woman. The "policy complication" either meant Bill Butler was talking through his hat in the first place or someone else had the job or the agency had lost the account. She cordially hoped it was the last.

That settled it.

Mr. Butler, whom she had met once and would never see again, had settled everything.

Her destiny was out of her hands. Now she had no choice but to let things happen and accept them.

She said goodbye to the 25 cities and the thousands of women who would be deprived of her sparkling personality and called the number on the matchbook Kip had given her.

After several rings, a sleepy, husky female voice purred hello.

"Kip?" it repeated the name languidly. "Ohhhhhh," it yawned. "He's still alseep . . . I think." It laughed indulgently to Melissa's annoyance.

She left word for him to call when he came to. Or was she too late? Had he met another girl at another bar who said yes at once instead of putting him off?

It was always like this. Her life was a multiple-choice test with no right answer. At first glance there always seemed to be so many answers, so many alternatives, so many different ways to solve her problems.

Yet, whichever one she chose was always, consistently wrong. She had an amazing aptitude for the near-answer, the shade of meaning that was almost right but in the long run was just as wrong as the completely wrong answer.

The result was the same whether you chose second best or last best, or refused to choose at all. There was after all only one right answer. You were supposed to know it when you found it. Melissa was afraid she had a short circuit somewhere inside her. Sometime or other she must have hit the right answer but no bells went off, no whistles shrieked. Nothing told her she had made it.

Had Max been the answer?

Was it going away with Kip?

Did someone older, like Walt, have it?

Or taking a sensible, routine job?

Or marrying Calvin?

She was going to Ingrid's for lunch to see the new clothes and the engagement ring Bernard had given her. This morning she would begin to pack her own clothes and make lists of things to do before the movers came on Thursday morning.

At about eleven, Max called. "I hope I didn't wake you up," he said in that defensive voice that enraged her. She let it pass. He wouldn't believe she'd been up since eight anyway. He was hemming and hawing which meant he had something to say.

"Melissa . . . I'm calling because I thought I would have time to get over there today or tomorrow to pick up those things—unless you've changed your mind about any of them—that is, I don't want them if you do . . ."

"I haven't changed my mind, Max. Come on over this afternoon. Late, because I'm having lunch out . . ."

"Well, the point is, I can't! What I mean is I'm up to my neck in regional meetings, unit sales managers, ticket agents. They're in from all over the country for conferences."

What did he want her to do? Pack his things and bring them over to his apartment strapped to her back? Or was he afraid to see her? She waited, silent.

In a rush, he said, "Well, the point is—and please don't be angry—my mother's in town for a few days. Staying at the apartment. Trying to make it habitable, she says, now that I'm a bachelor again—and, well, if you wouldn't mind too much, I wonder if you wouldn't mind if, well, she came over to get the things."

He was sending his mother! Little Max was going to be absent and instead of Mother writing a note, she was coming in person. The first time Melissa had met Mrs. Kempton was here, in this house, on that awful morning. For old times' sake, she should be wearing Max's bathrobe to greet the old bitch.

"I guess that'll be okay," she heard herself say. "I'm sure she knows better than you what you want and what you like. It will save you from making any more mistakes."

He got the message all right, but he was doing the Chamberlain bit. Peace at all costs.

"That's good of you, Melissa. I appreciate it. I'll tell her to come over first thing in the morning."

With his mother, first thing could mean dawn.

"Ask her to come after ten," she said, jumping at the chance to make a condition.

Ingrid didn't answer the downstairs bell but the front door was open. Melissa climbed the four marble flights of the converted townhouse to the upper duplex which began with a red enamel door festooned with a knot of daisies cascading from the knocker.

Puffing slightly from the ascent and a particularly tight girdle, she rang the bell and pulled on the knocker. From inside she could hear faint sounds and a rush of feet.

No one answered so she repeated her actions.

"Ingrid," she called. "Open up . . . it's me . . . Melissa . . . lunchtime . . . wakey-wakey . . ."

The door opened with a sudden wrench. Ingrid was in her favorite at-home costume, a paisley zip suit copied from the one Winston Churchill wore during the blitz. Past her, Melissa could see part of a man's torso sprawled on the couch at the far end of the living room.

"Melissa!" Ingrid shrieked joyfully, as if she had last seen her friend floating down the Orinoco on a runaway log. "I'd almost forgotten. Lunch. Of course. Lunch! *Quelle* Idiot am I!"

Emily Post? Amy Vanderbilt? What in God's name did she do now? Melissa was mortified at her own stupidity for coming upstairs and banging on the door as if the redcoats were coming. The honeymoon had obviously begun a couple of days early.

"As a matter of fact, I can't stay." She backed off. "I was in the neighborhood, just passing by, so I thought I'd drop by to tell you instead of calling. Must run."

Ingrid pulled her inside. "Don't be silly. I was expecting you. I want to see you. Guess who's here?" she asked in a gay falsetto.

Before Melissa could answer, Ingrid did it for her, pushing her into the living room.

"It's Philip. He came in for a cup of coffee. We were just talking about—real estate. I really must have that bell fixed."

Philip sprang to his feet.

"Hi, Missy. Late. Late. Late. Must go. Go. Go. 'Bye."

"Well, Philip," Melissa said, trying to gloss over her embarrassment, "now that Ingrid's getting married, I'm moving in here. So if you call this number and a strange woman answers, it's me."

"Married!" he said, startled. "Ingrid . . ?"

"Melissa! How could you! It's a secret!"

"Well," he smiled thinly. "So you're doing it at last. The lad with the Star of David on his bankbook I trust? He's a lucky man. Congratulations, Ingrid. Goodbye Melissa. Don't be too surprised if I *do* call."

The two women stood immobile until the door closed.

"Melissa! How could you?" Ingrid repeated, folding her arms and stamping her foot. "And making a pass at him right in front of me, too!"

"The question is, how could *you*?" Melissa flashed back. "Don't think I enjoy breaking in on this tender little love scene. It just never occurred to me that two days before your marriage you'd be warming up your motor with the also-ran."

"What are you talking about?"

Melissa lit a cigarette nervously.

"Are you kidding? I'm not exactly Rebecca of Sunnybrook Farm. I know how I look when I've been rolling in the hay. And that's how you look right this minute. Flushed. Sleepy. Bite marks on your neck. What the hell, Ingrid! I probably did you a favor. Philip would have to have known sooner or later and this way you didn't have to break it to him gently."

"I didn't want to break it to him gently. I was getting even with him today and you spoiled it. I made

203

a date with him for Friday night. Here. Quiet dinner at home. I told him to come at eight. With champagne. I was setting him up for the big evening. Then you were going to leave him a sweet little note—from me—saying sorry, dinner was off, because I was on my honeymoon. And you spoiled it! I could *kill* you!''

''But what's the point?''

''I wanted *him* to suffer for a change,'' Ingrid said, petulance distorting her mouth. ''Just once I wanted him to find out what it's like to want something and expect something and be kicked in the teeth.''

''Don't tell me you're marrying Bernard to get even with Philip?''

''Of course not! How can you say that! I love Bernard. I stopped getting even a long time ago.''

Melissa took her friend's hands and pressed them hard. ''I'm sorry if I said anything to upset you. A secret engagement is rough. You're only having a few days of wedding nerves.''

Ingrid hugged her.

''You're my dearest and best friend. The only time I can really let my hair down and be myself is with you. Sometimes I wish I'd stayed in the Bronx, eating spaghetti and getting fat. I'm sorry I snapped at you. So let's forget it or we'll both be crying.''

For lunch they ate an invention of Ingrid's, cold roast beef wrapped up in lettuce leaves and eaten with the fingers. It was a breadless sandwich, two hundred calories less than the standard model.

''You're not wearing your ring? Where is it? I want to see it.''

''Oh—I took it off. I didn't want to wear it because—well, it's a little too big and I don't want to lose it. Bernard's mother gave it to him when he was eighteen to give to his future wife. She doesn't know yet that he's given it to me. Ha!''

It was obviously a very old ring, an exquisite if elaborate platinum setting and a square cut diamond. On her hand it looked like an illustration from Godey's Lady's Book.

''Say, there's an inscription inside. 'To M.T. Forever and Ever.' What does it mean, Ingrid? Come on. What significance?''

''Oh, it's a silly name that he calls me sometimes.''

''What is it? I'm dying to know.''

''Oh, I can't tell you. It's too . . . well, silly. For an educated man, he can be awfully childish.''

''Oh, please. I won't tell. Cross heart. Hope die.''

''Well, all right . . . now, I warned you. M.T. stands for Mushy Tushy . . . Don't laugh. It's an endearing term in honor of my lovable rear end.''

''How wonderful!'' Melissa exploded. ''I love it! I've never heard that expression before!''

''I think it's Hebrew or Yiddish or something. I really never thought my posterior would be immortalized in platinum!''

At that moment, twelve blocks south and one block east of Ingrid's apartment, Walter Simpson rose from a snow-clad restaurant table, a figure of puzzled disbelief.

''Dana!'' he gasped as the familiar form of his wife paused and waited for him to seat her. ''I can't believe it's you!''

Dana smiled with great satisfaction, pleased with

her husband's reaction to how she looked, cheered by the knowing smiles from nearby tables.

"Yes, Walt. It's me," she said, conscious of the flattering pink glow cast on her face by the brim of her enormous pink straw skimmer. The black silk suit had long sleeves and a softly draped collar with an inset of pink at the neckline to soften the cruelties of age and booze on the throat and jaw. The young, coltish figure would never be restored but in its place stood a woman of abundance, a woman of the type revered by the French as being of *that certain age*.

"Am I late?" she asked in a voice that said of course she was late and wasn't he lucky she had remembered to come at all.

"No . . . no, of course not, darling—uh, Dana. Right on time. Right on the button. I was a little early. I wanted to be sure of a good table."

They looked at each other in silence. Both recognized simultaneously that their positions had unaccountably reversed. She who had worried all the way over in the cab about her makeup, about the new burnt almond hair rinse, about how hard it was going to be getting through lunch suddenly realized, "But this is going to be *easy*!"

He, who had dismissed the whole thing as something to be got over and done with and without a nasty scene suddenly knew with a fearsome omniscience, "This is going to be rough."

He ordered two martinis, very dry.

Dana touched his arm with a spotlessly gloved hand. "Thank you, no, Walter. Just tomato juice, please."

"Oh, sure, I get the picture." She looked magnificent but he could guess how she felt. "Want a little

206

worcestershire in it? Or some clam juice? Some people swear by clam juice. Better than hair of the dog . . . ''

"Just plain tomato juice," she repeated with exaggerated sweetness. "I don't happen to be in the need of a hangover remedy."

"Who said anything about being hung over?" he said, uneasy because that was exactly what he had been thinking.

"Well, we all know the therapeutic value of worcestershire and . . ."

"Only trying to be helpful. Want you to enjoy lunch."

There was nothing for her to say that would not be sarcastic. She had vowed ahead of time not to say one malicious word, not to be goaded into one reproach. She would have a friendly, expensive lunch. They would talk about lawyers and the weather. They would part friends.

Life was full of surprises. Here she was, lunching with a man for whom six months ago she would have died or spied or lied. Now he was a mere annoyance, like a runny nose, to be got rid of as quickly and efficiently as possible. Sitting across the table, he reminded her of their undergraduate days when he dogged her footsteps around campus, grateful when she let him buy her a hamburger.

Fred had picked her up out of the mud, washed her face and made her Queen of the Campus again. Who needed some snivelling undergrad when Professor Higgins himself wanted to keep her after school? School days were gone forever. *After school* meant all the years ahead.

"Dana. Believe it or not I'm tongue-tied. I don't know what to say."

"Pass the salt, Walt."

They laughed, relaxing slightly.

"I mean it," she said. "This salad needs some salt."

"Oh—yes. The salt." He searched among the jungle of mustard, sugar and seasonings, knocking it over in his haste.

"Quick—over your shoulder!" Dana commanded. "Make a wish!"

She pinched some of the salt with her fingers and threw it over her own shoulder, closing her eyes.

"What did you wish?" Walter asked gravely.

"Not supposed to tell."

"Please?"

"All right. I wished that you could find as much happiness as I have and that we can always be friends."

"You do look happy, Dana. You look so happy, you make me ashamed."

"Why? Aren't you relieved that you're not abandoning a wreck? That I'm not going to rot on some beach unless somebody takes me home for flotsam—or is it jetsam? I can never remember."

"Flotsam. Jetsam sinks."

"Well, I sank. About as low as you can sink. But I didn't like Davey Jones. That beard. *Icchhh*. Seaweed!" She laughed the tinkling melody that had once enslaved him and threatened to do so again.

"So," she shrugged with a tinge of triumph, "I'm back on dry land. I'm functioning. I've stopped drink ing and—other things. My skin, my figure are getting back to normal and life begins at 40-Plus.''

"There's a man?"

"There's a man."

"Do you love him?"

"Do you love someone who picked you up out of the gutter? In another few months you would have been visiting me in Bellevue!"

"That's not love," he said, angrily.

"Well, what *is* love?" she asked, matching his tone. "Trying to be a college girl for the rest of my life? Not having children because you wanted us to stay young and free as if we were still dating except that we could live together legally? Love is waking up every day with a good taste in your mouth, an appetite for what's waiting when you open your eyes. Fred loves me. He believes in me as a person. He needs me to fulfill himself not to decorate his apartment.''

"You haven't said you love him, Dana. You haven't said he's good in bed."

She colored and then sipped the water as if it were a new and unfamiliar liquid.

"You'd be amazed how many men are good in bed," she said quietly. "Being in bed is also reading and talking and learning about the other person. I'm glad you've changed your mind about the divorce. Is she pretty?"

"Is who pretty?"

"The girl who made you change your mind."

"Waiter—another martini and make it *dry* this time. If I wanted straight vermouth I would say so!"

He could not eat.

She continued her lunch, slowly, unperturbed, her eyes questioning.

He sipped the fresh drink with evident relief.

"Well, as a matter of fact, there is a girl."

"Ah," she said, triumphant but a little sad.

"No, it's not what you think. Her name is Melissa Kempton. She's divorced. Much younger than you," he said with unmeaning cruelty. "Pretty. Bright. Mixed up. She's being evicted from a little carriage house we've been commissioned to re-do. She interests me. She vexes me. But I'm not in love with her. In fact I just met her a few days ago. She's got a lot of wild ideas, that girl, but she's made me do some thinking."

"Remarkable girl."

"Tact is not her most outstanding feature. All she thinks about is herself and El Morocco but she's made me take a good clear look at myself . . . a sobering process I must say."

"You're still very attractive, Walter. The gray hair looks good. Like a whiskey ad. You really look fine," she said, as if to reassure him.

"Well, you won't find it hard to believe I've been making a colossal ass out of myself the past few months—chasing after ballet dancers, getting mixed up with hookers, taking advantage of cute little popsies out for a free meal. And what I've been doing to you is worse. Refusing to be a husband—but not wanting to cut you loose."

"And now?" she asked breathlessly.

"And now I've come like Abe Lincoln himself to set you free," he smiled wryly. "To secede from our union. You can have the divorce, Dana, anytime and

210

on your terms. Have a lawyer call my lawyer. We'll work out the details."

"Fine!" she said cheerfully. "That's very generous and sweet of you. I've heard I can get a Mexican divorce overnight."

"Overnight?"

He realized with a shock that she could be married to this Fred in a week—in days, even.

"Dana . . ." his hand reached for her, stopped an inch short of the mark.

Like the century plant, some women's flowering waits for one special day to burst forth in lavish splendor. This was Dana's day and all at once she knew it.

"Yes, Walt . . ?"

"There's so much I want to tell you, to ask you. So many things we never seemed able to talk about before but now I think we can."

She looked at her watch.

"We haven't much time. Fred is picking me up here at two."

"You didn't want to spend much time with me, did you? I could tell when you came in. You've been counting the minutes. What's wrong? Do I frighten you, Dana?"

"No," she said slowly. "Fred seemed to think I'd need some moral support. It's comforting to have someone worried about you."

"Do you want a guardian or a lover?"

She picked up her gloves and bag.

"I think I'll wait for Fred outside."

"Oh, please—I'm sorry, Dana. I lost my temper. It's only that I feel that I've found you again and not only that, I've found a new me. It breaks me up when you back away from me. I can't believe that you're afraid of me.''

"I'm not afraid," she insisted, tears filling her eyes.

"Dana . . ."

"What?"

"What time is it?"

"Ten of."

"Dana . . . please let's get out of here and go somewhere when we can talk. Please . . ."

Long ago, someone had told her to find a man who loved her for herself not her beauty. Fred was that man. He had found her, recognized the delicate porcelain under the layer of grime.

By contrast, Walter was the shadow man lurking behind the girl in the scare advertisements. Warning her not to be drab, mousy, overweight. Urging her to be slim, vivacious, glowing with sex appeal. The shadow man didn't pitch in and help. He stayed in the half-light and passed judgment.

She put on her gloves, slowly working each finger into place. It was a female delaying action, calculated to madden and disrupt. He remembered Melissa doing it the first day they met.

"Dana . . . I'm not asking you. I'm begging you. Please, please come with me. This minute."

She leaned toward him with eyes made larger by sadness.

"No," she whispered, barely audible. "No, no, *no*! You don't seem to understand, Walt. I have an *appointment* at two o'clock. You may not think it's very important to keep *appointments*. But I do. And so does Fred. I like having someone who is punctual,

212

reliable—and dependable. I like to know, without one little gnawing doubt in the pit of my stomach, that when the clock says two o'clock, Fred will be here. On the dot! You're the most handsome man I know, Walt. Even now, after all these years and all the ugliness, it prickles my spine to look at you. Even when you were rotten, I thought you were wonderful. But having a husband who's a professional hotshot with a smooth line and a bag of tricks is not for me. I'm too old. I'm a middle-aged woman and I want a middle-aged man, not a perennial boy. Some married men complain their wives haven't grown up with them. Well, I've grown past you. We're in different age levels. Excuse me, I'm going to the Powder Room to fix my face. I'll say goodbye now because I won't have time to come back.''

Walt felt his taut, tanned body crumple inside his continental suiting. Dana had it all wrong. Sure, he was the heel that all the swinging chicks loved, the no-good rover with the hideaway wife, but couldn't she see he had left her for the last time, that he had come back to her for keeps? Why was she doing this to him?

Still another few blocks away, on an almost direct line to the west, Max Kempton had escaped from his regional confabs long enough to meet his mother for a quick coffee break.

"You're sure you don't mind, Mother? Going over to Melissa's? She said about ten tomorrow morning would be fine."

"Of course I don't mind. Whatever will make you comfortable is no sacrifice for me. I suggested it,

213

didn't I? You were going to let her have everything. You're much too generous with her, Max. So far as I'm concerned, it's still your house and your belongings."

"If you have that attitude, maybe you'd better not go, Mother. Melissa is plenty upset about having to move. I don't want the two of you in a hair-pulling match over an ashtray."

"You'll have no worry there, I assure you. I can conduct myself with the proper decorum. Whatever cruel, inhuman things she may say will go in one ear and out the other. So far as I'm concerned, Melissa never wanted to get along with me, never tried to be a good daughter-in-law."

He sighed and stirred his coffee.

"You two just started off on the wrong foot. It was nobody's fault, just a big mistake all around."

"The mistake was your ever marrying her. What can you expect from someone who gads about Europe all by herself, who's rude to her stepfather, that charming man? And when I think that she didn't have enough respect for herself or for you to wait until—"

"Look. It's late. I have only a few minutes. There's another conference at two-thirty. This is our only chance to talk because tonight I'll be out late with the Chicago contingent. They want to do the town. So let's have a quiet cup of coffee and not rake up the past. Now it's all settled, isn't it? You'll go to the house tomorrow and take whatever you think will fit into the apartment. Mark it and the movers will deliver it to me on Thursday when they take the rest of the things to storage. And—try and be nice to Melissa, will you, Mother?"

"Nice? That's all everybody is to Melissa. Nice and sweet and understanding and generous. All she does is sit around all day spending your money. Not even a job. How long are you going to keep on supporting her? For the rest of her life? So far as I'm concerned she's a parasite! What did she ever give you that she can sit back? A happy home? A child? Someone to carry your name? No, my poor, trusting darling. She gave you nothing!"

"She wanted a child, Mother. Give her credit for that. I tried to give it to her but I couldn't."

'What do you mean you couldn't? A big, strong, healthy boy like you? There must be something wrong with *her*! Things to wrong with a girl who doesn't respect herself. Why, a woman in our club read us a summary of the Kinsey report on women that said most prostitutes are sterile! What do you think of that!"

"I think you've gone too far," he said into his coffee. "There's nothing wrong with her."

"There must be something wrong. Did you go to a doctor? Did you ever get *her* examined by a doctor? Why didn't you confide in your mother, Max? She tried to turn you away from me, I could tell. So far as I'm concerned, there's something wrong with her and I have half a mind to tell her so myself."

"I wouldn't do that if I were you."

"Why on earth not? If there *is* something wrong with her then you could have gotten an annulment on the grounds of not living up to the marriage contract, not having a family. Then you wouldn't have to pay her a dime."

"Mother, in the simplest possible language I want you to do two things for me. One is to stop concerning yourself with what I do or do not do with my money. Second is not to broach the subject of babies with Melissa."

"Why? Why? Why?" Her tight gray curls quivered with indignation.

She could not let well enough alone.

"Because you're liable to get a shock."

His mother smiled. "You forget that while I'm your mother, I'm also a married woman. I've had children. I know the facts of life. I won't shock that easily."

Now was as good a time as any.

"Melissa did become pregnant."

That shut her up.

"You might as well know, Mother. You're part of it. In fact, Melissa blames you for the whole thing. Melissa was pregnant before we were married." He raced on without a pause. "I know how conventional you are, how upset you were to find Melissa with me that morning. We decided there were certain things we owed our parents, or rather I thought so, and a fancy, sociable wedding is one of them. We thought we were sophisticated world travelers indulging the older generation. We thought having babies was pure mechanics, that we just had to keep on—doing what we were doing—push a button and out would come baby, cradle and all. So—"

"So—?" she asked, her face contorted, knowing the answer.

"So—we got rid of it."

"You mean—" something compelled her to say the word, "abortion."

Max nodded.

"At the time, it seemed like the best way out what with all the wedding plans and you the Mother of Virtue. However much Melissa may rail against her family, it's just an act. She wants to be part of them. She wants their approval even when she's behaving as badly as she can."

He noted with detachment that his mother looked faint.

"God help me!" she whispered. "She's robbed me of a grandchild and she's blaming it on me! I didn't tell her to be shameless and vile and desecrate the marriage vows, did I?"

"Mother, you make me sick. My wife had her insides scraped out because I was worried about what you would think. You're not thinking of her or me and what we've missed by not having a child. You're only thinking of yourself because there's one less grandchild to spoil!"

"How dare you speak to your mother that way! I have grandchildren, two beautiful babies. My daughter has given me what my son has not!"

"Sure. And your daughter and her husband live in Seattle, Washington. Why do you suppose they moved out there? I'll tell you. To get three thousand miles away from you. I have a pretty smart sister. When they come east once a year to see you, everybody's happy and has a wonderful time. The rest of the year they stay out of your way."

"For your information, I urged them to move to Seattle. They would have been foolish to turn down such a lucrative offer."

If that was his mother's fantasy he would let her have it.

"I'm afraid you and I are stuck with each other, Mother—maybe for life. This will give us something to talk about. I don't think I'll be getting married again. In fact, I have one more piece of shocking news for you, Mother. I'm still in love with Melissa. I hate her for what she's doing to herself, but I love her despite it. If I knew how to do it, I'd try to make her come back to me."

"You'll do no such thing," she remonstrated, her power returned.

"No! But not because of you. But because of my very basic, neurotic inability to function as a husband."

"What do you mean?" she rushed to his defense as always. His champion. His cheering squad of one. Give 'im the axe!

"So far as I'm concerned," he mimicked her expression, "you're old enough to be told. I am a frightened schoolboy. And in the words of a schoolboy, *I can't get it up!*"

Crosstown and uptown to the first point of the triangle, Melissa was lying on Ingrid's bed, cradling a mug of coffee as her friend paraded up and back in her trousseau.

"Twenty bucks for this one pair of shorts! I could have gone to Ohrbach's or wholesale and got four pair for that money. But there's something very satisfying about twenty-dollar shorts."

"I know what you mean. And they look wildly expensive, too."

"Yes—be perfect for Palm Springs later on—unless we tour the Greek Islands. Then it'll be more fun to go native."

"When are you going to let Bernard work so he can earn all this money you're spending?"

"Oh, he comes into an enormous trust fund next year. His grandfather left it for him. My grandfather left me an enamelled Madonna."

Melissa flopped over on her belly.

"Maybe I better skip the java. I've been drinking too much coffee lately. Had the most horrible nightmare last night. Mothers chasing me and babies with men's faces. It was awful. I woke up panting and screaming as if I'd been running for miles and do you know that grate outside my front door? I was down on my hands and knees, shaking the bars like a madwoman, begging to be let in!" She shuddered. "Still can't shake it."

"Have a tranquillizer. Do you good. Must have been something you ate. I haven't had dreams like that since I stopped eating pasta. Speaking of nerves, how's your voodoo coming? Kill anybody lately?"

"That's not funny, Ingrid. Max's mother is coming over in the morning to get some of his things; the coward. I'm worried that I might get a sudden impulse to stab her with a hat pin."

Ingrid laughed. "Then all that hot air would come shooting out. Great! You'll be able to slide her out under the door."

Ingrid was off to Rubenstein's for a pedicure and massage to go with her new wardrobe so Melissa returned home to the tedious business of packing and deciding what to store and what to give away.

The Kipper had called but when she tried him again, the same langorous voice answered. Didn't he ever get out of bed?

Dominic had not checked in. He probably wouldn't. Not for a few days. Maybe not ever again. Not after being thrown out. T.S.

As she put the phone down, it rang.

"Hello, Kip?"

"No—it's me. Ellis."

"Oh, hi. Was expecting someone else."

Ellis chattered brightly about the children and the house until Melissa suddenly remembered she was peeved at her sister.

"What's the big idea siccing mother on me last night? She did everything but sing 'The Star Spangled Banner.' I expressly asked you not to tell her about the eviction."

"Oh, I'm sorry, Missy. I told her not to mention it to you. It just slipped out. She called me to say how worried she was about you living all alone in the house and before I knew it I told her not to worry about you being alone in the house much longer. She wormed it all out of me. You know how mother is."

Melissa knew.

But that obviously wasn't why Ellis had called. She never made a toll call from Long Island without a good reason, especially when they'd seen each other as recently as Sunday.

She had been stalling. Now she plunged in, always the awkward thrasher when she was in over her head.

"Missy, I have something to tell you. It's very embarrassing for me. But—" in a rush "—I'm afraid I have to take back the invitation."

220

"What invitation?"

What was she talking about?

"The invitation to stay with us when you move. You know . . ."

Melissa had dismissed the unlikely possibility the moment it was suggested; she was genuinely surprised that her sister seriously believed she would move to the boon docks.

"Oh, but Ellis . . ."

"Oh, Missy. Please forgive me and try and understand. John says the children have a set routine that shouldn't be disturbed. He thinks the household should run smoothly, on an even keel, that we have to avoid any remote chance of divided loyalty or anything like that . . . why, John says . . ."

So Jovial John was afraid to have her in his home. She migt corrupt the children.

Or him?

Never had she felt such loathing for this man nor such jealousy of her sister whose mate reared up like primitive man to protect her cave against all intruders.

"It's okay, Ellis. Don't give it another thought. I wasn't planning on coming anyway. I thought I'd made that clear. You know how I feel about suburbia. Squaresville. Anyway, I'd be afraid to sleep in your house. I might start talking and then you would have to rush to the phone and report everything I said to Mother. 'I Squealed On My Sister For The F.B.I.' "

"Oh, Missy! Stop. Don't be angry. Please . . ."

"I'm packing now, Ellis. Give my love to the girls."

She hung up, shaking with rage.

When you came right down to it, nobody really wanted you.

She wondered about Walter. He hadn't called or come around. Maybe he was waiting until she left on Thursday. Their meetings were not exactly amicable. He made the glamorous things she did seem pointless and childish, her outlook on men and love unrealistic and selfish. It was as well if they didn't see each other. He wouldn't approve of her going away with Kip, assuming Kip still wanted her. Not that Walt would do anything about it of course, like maybe try and stop her or anything. Oh, no—but he wouldn't approve. Conscience didn't advise; it merely judged.

Men who set themselves up as arbiters of your personal life were invariably moralizers.

—"Why are you wasting yourself on this or that?"

—"Tempus is fugiting and you're not getting any younger, you know."

—"Why isn't a nice girl like you married and having children?"

*Why, indeed?*

They never had an alternative to suggest, except possibly a transient form of solace, with them, of course.

Kip's call jarred her back to reality. He was glad she had decided to go with him. At least, *he* was enthusiastic about their future together, brief though it might be. As proof of how sure he was of her, he had cadged an assignment from *Look* magazine to photograph an American girl wearing whatever native fashions they could find on their South American travels. She would be the Yanqui, of course, and receive a modelling fee as well.

222

Would this merriment never cease?

The current plan called for it to begin the following Tuesday. South America, take it away. *Aqui se habla Español* and all that. The Portugese fishermen of Cape Cod were divine. She wondered if the Brazilian variety would be as exciting. This time she would make Kip jealous. You learn a lot in four years.

It was too good to be true. She could hardly wait to tell Ingrid she was going to be a fashion model, too—and for *Look* magazine! She must remember to get some professional pointers. Ingrid was always talking about her hip bone and there's some secret way to tuck in your elbow but now Melissa couldn't remember just what you did.

It wouldn't matter too much. Kip was such a great photographer he gave everyone a soul. He would capture the spirit of the clothes and the geography with such force that her physical imperfections wouldn't matter. They wouldn't show.

An even more delirious idea struck her. Maybe she'd be on the cover. Most of Kip's stories made the cover. Kip would reveal the inner Melissa, the driving passion and conflicting desires that set her apart from others. He might even show her a part of herself she didn't know existed and give her a new dimension.

Then, *Look* magazine would get all excited—postpone a Grace Kelly cover and use her instead! Letters . . . marriage proposals . . . movie offers would pour into *Look*'s offices. She would be rich, famous, loved. Thanks to the Kipper.

Oddly enough, fashion modelling had never figured among Melissa's dreams of glory. As a child, her ambitions had changed as regularly as the neighborhood movie. Dance Hall Girl With Heart Of Gold (Ann Sheridan); Heiress Who Learns True Meaning of Love (Katherine Hepburn); Secretary Who Marries Rich And Handsome Boss (Ginger Rogers); Hoofer Who Becomes Overnight Sensation (Betty Grable) and of course Bitch On Wheels Who Drives Men Mad (Bette Davis).

Her favorite characterization was of the ugly duckling who became a swan by taking off her glasses. She hadn't needed glasses but bought a pair of frames at Woolworth's to test their efficacy at a party. Nothing was supposed to happen until, magically, she took them off. But the boys didn't know the rules. They thought the glasses were the funniest idea they ever saw. They fought over her bodily to try on the frames and mimic various teachers. Suddenly she was being hailed as a sparkling wit and undisputed belle of the gathering, though not in quite the way she had planned.

The darkened movie theatre with its ornate carvings and stained glass had been her cathedral; her regular place of worship, her fountain of ideas. It never let her down. It soothed and inspired and excited and calmed. It opened new avenues of thought, new areas to conquer. It showed the many, many ways to right-eousness for the sake of a happy ending.

Despite a once-a-week rule, most weeks she went both Saturday and Sunday afternoons, sometimes starting at ten in the morning. Admittedly, New York is a cultural paradise of museums, children's concerts, special exhibits and historical buildings but since these required the planning and supervision of an interested adult, Melissa was encouraged in her preference for films.

The neighborhood parents took turns shepherding groups of children on weekend excursions but the group system was purely reciprocal. Twice, Claire had agreed to take a party of six to the Hayden Planetarium. Twice she had come down with a headache at the last minute, leaving a half dozen brushed and ribboned dynamos scuffling their Mary Janes with no choice but the movies for which Melissa's mother so generously offered to treat.

Melissa was a fair child. She could readily understand why the other mothers might not want to drag her along. In fact she saved herself from possible rejection by announcing that she preferred the movies to any boring trips around town.

Often, her movie privileges were taken away in midweek as punishment for an infraction of household laws such as leaving dirty dishes in the sink. They were always restored, by Saturday morning the latest, as Melissa knew they would. Having her mope around the house all weekend with nothing to do was more punishment for the family than for her.

Once inside the theater she would sneak up to the balcony and sit in the last row, pulling at a chocolate cigarette until an alert usher hauled her back downstairs to the children's section. She vaguely envied the older boys and girls necking and wrestling on all sides of her. One afternoon, when she was eleven, a short boy with a leather jacket and a real cigarette in his mouth sat down next to her and put his hand on her leg. Paralyzed with uncertainty, she was saved by the usher's flashlight and his tired voice, "Back to the Children's Section. I'm tired of telling you."

Her earliest idol had been Jeanette MacDonald in

a movie about the settlement of Louisiana. To the annoyance of the other patrons, she sang along with Jeanette in a high, piercing voice. She soon dropped singing as her life's work because even at home in the tiled soundbox of her bathroom, her tone was unbearably flat. Next, Sonia Henie's career hung in jeopardy for three painful weeks on the frozen tennis courts at 94th Street and West End Avenue. She enjoyed the climactic sprained ankle because it meant she could wear a cast and limp and be excused from gym and ride the school elevator reserved for teachers. It also meant she could give away the figure skates which had never fit her very well in the first place, having been handed down by an older cousin.

In the war between Shirley Temple and Jane Withers, she sided with Jane. Jane wasn't really a rat. Melissa understood her. Who could blame her for being mean and nasty when Shirley Temple was so adorable and had so much talent and everybody loved her more?

After seeing the Andy Hardy series, she was genuinely shocked when her first boy friends did not behave the way Andy Hardy did in a parked car. They didn't just kiss her and go daffy and say she was wonderful and would she go steady and to the big dance. They said she was a lousy sport. Nor was her family life even remotely as gay as that of her cinematic contemporaries. Maybe, she had concluded, it was because she lived in an apartment instead of a private house in a small town.

A fashion model was slim and angular. With any willpower at all she could lose ten pounds before next week. Looking in the mirror and mentally airbrushing away the more pronounced curves, she decided not to tell Ingrid about her good fortune. With Kip, the whole thing could evaporate minutes before plane time. Explaining why you *didn't* do something was often more difficult than explaining why you *did*. Ingrid would be gone anyway. If the trip came through as planned, she would leave a note.

At four o'clock she stopped her packing halfway between old ski-pants and a collection of eyebrow pencils in a Marshall Field gift box. If only she had one of those silent, understanding old Nannies who refused to leave her side even though she couldn't afford to pay her now that the family fortunes were low.

*"Nanny, you really mustn't do all this packing in one day. Remember you're ninety-eight and you have a heart condition."*

*"Now, now, Miss Melissa child, when your father and mother died, they made me promise to take care of you. And that's what I'm doing. Now you go along, have your fun and let old Nanny take care of the packing. Now run along."*

She walked the six blocks to the cold-water flat shared by Quentin and Calvin, the latter having asked her up for tea and a look at some of his new designs. She hoped Quentin wouldn't be there. He made her skin itch.

The apartment was actually two railroad flats combined into one and comprised the entire top floor of a dilapidated tenement. Each ran the length of the building, three rooms one behind the other like railroad cars, with a door to the landing at either end, adding up to four doors in total or an ideal set for a Marx Brothers comedy. Surrounded by the one large apartment, the outside landing became a private atrium, painted pink, the safety rail draped in cork-strewn fishnet.

The controlled rent was $22 a month for each partment or a grand total of $44 for six rooms in a neighborhood where one-room apartments with pullman kitchens were being grabbed for a hundred and fifty as bargains. The term "cold water" actually meant hot water but no heat, a problem easily overcome with electric heaters. Steam heat is so drying to the membranes. The original bathroom facilities were a bathtub that a previous tenant had used for coal, and a hall privy.

Quentin had begun modestly, his only modest action in a life dedicated to extravagance, with one of the apartments which he found by chance the very day he arrived in New York from Iowa just before the war. He had a small allowance, a small beard and the hearty wish of his family that he stay in New York, or anywhere else, for good. A hundred years earlier he would have been sent to Australia or the East as a remittance man along with the black sheep and skeletons of other families.

His unfortunate relationship with the mayor's son had been fortunate only in that it was the mayor's son. Legalities were forgotten in the haste of speeding Quentin on his way to bigger, better and further things. Unruffled, he regarded the course of events as divine providence plotting on his behalf.

The rent in 1941 had been $18 a month and he had had to share the outside toilet with the family of six

228

in the other apartment. Fastidiously clean by nature, Quentin carried a bottle of Lysol solution every time urgency forced him to use the facilities. As time went on, he routinized his daily function so as to be elsewhere.

Diabetes having kept him out of the service, he continued his studies at the Parsons School of Fashion and by war's end he had begun to establish himself as a designer of sportswear for women who wanted to look sportive without having to risk movement.

Like other successful purveyors of personal service, he established a thrilling rapport with each member of his clientele. Women liked him, trusted his taste. They recognized instinctively that he was on their side with ingenious new ways to attract men. If he charged much too much and made them wait much too long, what did it matter?

His prices were exorbitant, sometimes beyond reason, his theory being that his clientele was not looking for bargains but romance, excitement and the ecstasy of spending too much money. The more outrageous the price, the more they wanted to pay it.

To be fair, his workmanship was superb, his instinct for each woman infallible. He supervised every fitting himself, adjusting each detail with mounting frenzy and always—it was his most clever device—making a last-minute impulsive change, inspired by the lady herself.

In 1946, by a stroke of good luck and a fifty dollar bill in the right palm, his neighbors' lease was not renewed and Quentin expanded his living quarters.

Six rooms is a lot for one person. He invited a young interior decorator to share them. Together, they knocked plaster off the walls to expose the red brick, tore out rotting windows and partitions and fitted out one room as a bathroom which took its inspiration from Roman pornography, and another as a kitchen which also would have pleased classical appetites.

With the interior decorator's professional discount and Quentin's eye for the bizarre, they left the bare brick in one room and mounted an elephant head on it, flanked with antique guns. They lined another room with red velvet and hung it with gilt-framed mirrors to reflect the Restoration bed which had a gargoyle panel that twisted to reveal a carved crucifix. The bed filled the room, its canopy just missing a candelabra chandelier whose crystals tinkled at the slightest breeze.

The living room—or Reception Room, as Quentin called it—was actually the two end rooms combined, the windows converted into one long picture window, the two fire escapes joined with an iron catwalk holding a jungle of rhododendron to give the feeling of a garden outside.

All in all, it was quite an apartment. Elaborate! Unique! A conversation piece for clients who vied for the privilege of being asked there for private consultation. While his Park Avenue salon was ornate and featured a Senegalese boy in fuschia livery to serve coffee and cocktails, it was not quite so ''inside'' as the fabled apartment.

When the interior decorator finished the job, to the neglect of his own business, Quentin told him to move. People were saying they were queer, he explained. He would have none of that talk.

He had lived more or less alone since until he met

Calvin at the bar at P.J. Clarke's. Calvin was a fresh kid. He didn't look at Quent with those simpering moo-cow eyes of so many of the new crop of boys, especially the ones who camped on Third Avenue at midnight waiting for a pick-up. Ever since some columnist had renamed it Queen's Boulevard, Third Avenue had become cheap. Quentin avoided it as much as possible now.

Calvin had been homeless but he wasn't begging. If Quent wanted to put him up for the night, okay.

"I'm up for grabs," Calvin had said and Quent still tingled at the recollection. "Some old broad told me I looked like her son. She gave me her address and told me to come up after midnight. If nothing better comes along before midnight, I'm Cinderella."

Quentin had taken him home.

Melissa stood ankle deep in the zebra skin rug, wondering if the living beast had been a pederast while Calvin went for some coffee. She had never seen the living room by daylight. By night it had the garish splendor of a Cocteau aberration. Now the harsh green sofa hurt her eyes, the zebra hair stuck to her shoes, a portrait of Quentin hung in baroque and lighted with reverence, gave her the creeps.

"Instant coffee, sweetie. Hope you don't mind. Quent bought these croissants—pure French affectation—but I hid them away with my tennis socks just to give him a hard time. He was *puce* this morning, in a regular snit, tearing the place apart. Butter and jam? This is one hell of an English tea. Instant coffee and French croissants from a phoney Italian bakery."

"Watch out. I think Quentin is standing behind the portrait watching us. His eyes just moved."

231

"Dorian Gray. I swear it gets uglier every time I look at it. And so does Quentin. He thinks it makes him look Byronic. Byron would turn over in his grave."

"None of that sniping now. Is all peaceable among haute couture?"

"Is cold war. Velly cold. Think any time now guns go boom boom. Kill Quentin dead dead. Most tellible accident. Vello solly."

She had been to the apartment only once before at Calvin's invitation to a Hallowe'en costume party. She had come as Salome with a paste diamond in her navel and a handful of chiffon scarves draped from a barette on top of her head.

She had known something was wrong the minute she arrived. Quent, dressed as a bullfighter but looking like a Disney picador, came up to her after the Senegalese boy had let her in but stopped short when she introduced herself.

"Of course," he said, turning his back to greet a heavily rouged ballerina dressed completely in pink. "Calvin said he asked you. Have fun."

Calvin in a Mack Sennet bathing costume rescued her then and stayed at her side, mixing her into conversations, signalling for drinks and refreshments. As her eyes became accustomed to the cavernous light and the smarting mists of incense, she slowly realized she was the only bonafide female there.

"I'm sorry, Melissa," he said, when she left early. "When I asked you, I just didn't think."

As she ate her croissant and sipped the coffee, Calvin brought out his designs, some in muslin, some translated into fabric.

232

"They're wonderful, Calvin! I want them all." Her admiration was sincere. This confused, frightened boy had somehow injected a grace and purity of line into his creations which said at once they would flatter and glorify the wearer.

"Well . . . when does the world get a look-see? When will you show your first collection?"

He bit his lower lip.

"I'm going to burn them all. Nothing is going to happen. Quentin will see to that. He won't even discuss it with me. He's plotting behind my back. I can't stand people being against me. You know how influential he is. Women listen to him. Some of them obey him faster than their stupid husbands who are stupid enough to pay his bills. And he's head cutie-poo when it comes to the kiss of death. Christ! A few acid comments from him and I might as well close up before I open. Hell, I can't open. I'll never open. Let's forget it."

"But what about your workroom?" she asked with concern. "Aren't you going ahead with it?"

"Afraid not," he said, staring out the window. "The renting agent's been after me to sign or he'll give it to someone else. I told him to give it to some deserving heterosexual."

"Calvin!" she cried. "Oh, Calvin, you can't give in to him. I've just got an idea. Listen. Thursday I'll be moving into Ingrid's. She's getting married but it's a secret and all a big muchness so you mustn't tell but anyway—it's a big duplex with beautiful furniture and lots of room and sun. She likes you very much. Why, we've even talked about going into business with you. So you can use Ingrid's apartment! I'm going away next week—that's a secret, too, so you can move in and fix things to suit you. It'll be marvellously chic—on top of an old town house. Marble stairs and all. Just great!''

Dead air response. Calvin did not share her enthusiasm.

"It wouldn't work. I'm cooked. I need lots of open space for bolts of material and a sewing machine and mirrors and what not. I can't just take over an apartment with all the furniture and work around it. I may just peddle these designs to Seventh Avenue and let someone else have the joy of selling them.''

"Sure—for peanuts. In some sleazy material. Part of what you do is in the fabric and the way you manipulate it and make it spring to life. Like that stuff over there! It's positively creamy. What is it?''

"Oh, that's Quent's—a new kind of silk brocade that has no stiffness. He's going to make a brunch romper out of it or something. Boy, couldn't I make something doozie out of it? Stand up, Melissa. You feel like being a model for a few minutes?''

She longed to tell him about the South American story but she had long ago learned that some things keep better until after they happen. *If* they happen.

"Come on. I think I'll drape you. It isn't often that I get a whack at a living model. Those dressmaker dummies have no personality whatever.''

"Do I take off my dress?'' This was going to be fun.

"Have to. Just slip it off and get up on this stool. I'll get my pins. Got a great idea.''

"I feel like a department store dummy waiting for the window dresser,'' she said, thinking how odd it was to be standing with her dress off while a young man draped fabric around her, pinning here, smoothing there, touching her with haste and meaning and a familiarity with body structure if only in terms of planes and convolutions.

She had never had a male dressmaker. Except for the doctor and a French masseur in St. Tropez, men who had touched her meant it. Here were strong, quick, artistic fingers flitting over her yet she had no reaction other than the sweetness of being part of a creative work.

"It's beginning to take shape," Calvin said, his ears pink with excitement. "Designing should be done this way, working with the fabric alone and a live, human figure. The hell with sketches. The sketches come later. Afterwards. Not before. This way the cloth moves freely almost as if it had a will of its own and all I have to do is watch it and control it . . ."

The door opened.

Quentin stood, unbelieving, his walking stick and gloves held straight out, his Edwardian suit flaring from the waist, unmarred by the smallest crease or wrinkle. He had trained his Senegalese to keep a small iron ready to press his suits right on him when he arrived in the morning and before leaving the shop for any reason whatever. If possible, he walked home and to appointments to avoid the crushing hazards of taxis.

"What the hell do you think you're both doing—and in my apartment? Ah, I see what happened to the croissants. Did she take you to bed to get you to find them, Calvin? I see you save all your cheap little tricks for my benefit."

235

Melissa said nothing. Being caught with a man by the man's protector was a new situation.

"Shut up. Genius at work!" Calvin continued to drape, blithely affecting disdain of the older man's anger but Melissa could feel his fingers shaking.

"Not with *my* fabric you don't! That cost me twelve dollars a yard which is twelve dollars more than I've seen from your pocket in quite some time. Amateurs should work in muslin—or crepe paper!"

He stood close behind Calvin who was gravely tracing the flow of the bodice. Melissa stared down helplessly at both heads.

Quent pushed Calvin aside. "Didn't you hear me? I said amateurs should work in muslin! I'll take it now if you don't mind. I don't want any messy pin pricks in it."

"Speaking of pricks, you're the prick!" Calvin muttered, shoving him back.

Quentin grabbed the loose end of the fabric and pulled hard, sending the pins in all directions and knocking Melissa off her perch.

Calvin pushed him again.

"Don't touch that, you bastard. It's my design. It's better than anything you can do. I haven't finished it, you jealous shit! I have to make a sketch before I undo it."

Melissa was still very much encased in the fabric, the key pins having stayed put. To pull it off would destroy Calvin's idea. On the other hand Quentin looked as if he might kill them both with his walking stick.

"Get that off her!" Quent screamed, lunging at Calvin, flailing the air with his stock. A Chinese porcelain crashed to the floor. He jumped up and down on the pieces.

"You no-good thief! You lousy little shit! What else have you been stealing while I'm not here? I notice that's my shirt you're wearing. Take it off!"

"Okay!" Calvin shouted back. "Melissa, unpin yourself and get out of here or you're liable to get hurt when I kill this son of a bitch!"

He unbuttoned the shirt and punched his scissors through it. "There! There! There!" he shouted, slashing it into jagged strips.

Melissa struggled into her dress, the disputed fabric at her feet. Calvin speared it with the point of his scissors and threw it at Quentin.

"And *there*! Take it. It stinks anyway."

Quent flung it from his distastefully. "You're right, it does stink. It stinks from you and her. It's contaminated with the cheap perfume your over-sexed girl friend uses. I'll never forgive you for doing that to my shirt. Not in a million years."

"Sod you!" Calvin shouted.

Melissa could see he was scared to death but game for a fight.

"Come on, Calvin. Walk me home." She picked up the brocade. "If you guys don't want this, I do."

To the bystander, the spoils.

"Take it!" Quentin snarled. "Take everything you see. You come here on a raiding party behind my back. Take him, too. He's no bargain. He never bathes or changes his underwear. He's a cheat and a liar . . ."

Frenzied now, Quentin knocked over a lamp and kicked the stool on which Melissa had been standing clear across the room. Calvin ran into the next room,

Quentin behind him. She could hear scuffling and yelling and a new kind of cursing.

Calvin returned, panting and clutching a folded shirt in his hand. He smiled weakly. "The man is sick, off his nut. Let's blow this coop. I'll put the shirt on downstairs."

Quentin plunged back into the room behind the antique elephant gun torn from its moorings in the brick-lined study.

"I'm going to kill both of you," he screeched his back to the outside door.

Calvin dashed. Melissa followed. They ran through the other rooms, skirting the restoration bed, ducking under the hanging trunk of the deceased elephant, through the sunken and happily empty bathtub and out the door at that end of the landing, with Quentin inches behind yelling, "Stand still. Stand still. I don't want to hurt my furniture!"

Laughing hysterically in short convulsive gasps, they streaked across the landing and clattered down the steep iron stairs. Melissa's shoe came off and plunged down the stairwell.

Above them, Quentin stood, bellowing incoherently, pointing the gun down at them.

"My God! It isn't loaded, is it?" Melissa asked breathlessly as they reached the street level.

"God alone knows. People in the papers are always saying, 'Officer, I didn't know it was loaded.' *Bam*! Guts all over the floor."

Next to the stairwell and out of range of any possible stray bullet, they paused for breath. Calvin hastily put on the shirt. Melissa found her shoe and slipped into it.

A small boy, about three years old, with a filthy face and hands, peered out from a doorway. They could hear a woman's voice beyond him calling, "Harry, shut the door or I'll beat your ass. You hear me? Shut the door. It's making a draft."

Harry closed the door behind him, walked solemnly past his two observers to the sagging wooden balustrade and urinated against it, looking to them for approval.

"Oh, God. Fresh air! Please!" Melissa cried.

Hand-in-hand like school children, they ran through the late afternoon streets, dodging traffic, snaking through homeward-bound crowds.

"Let's forget what happened. Let's pick up where we left off, Calvin," she said once they had gained sanctuary. "There's no point losing the design altogether. We have the material. I have some pins floating around somewhere. I'll put on some draping music and you can drape. It'll be fun for me, too."

Looking down on his bent crewcut head a few minutes later, she asked, "Where to from here, Calvin? You're certainly not going back to the wax museum."

"I have to go back," Calvin said, not looking up. "He knows it and I know it. He's having lunch with Cora tomorrow. He'll tell her not to help me if I don't make up with him."

When he looked up, his face was ashen, a living deathmask, his eyes sightless tarpits, burnt out, seeing nothing and everything too clearly.

"The truth is—I can't break away from him. He's too strong. I'm too weak."

He stuck her with a pin but she didn't budge.

"I'm a worm, Melissa, a crawly, creepy worm. In

239

fact, when I die worms won't even want me. Do you know what he made me do the other morning after I slept here? He made me get down on my knees and apologize and promise on the Bible not to do it again and I *promised*! I've been kidding myself that I'm a man. The only way I can tell is my birth certificate says so. Maybe I'm like all those kids in Gilbert and Sullivan. Mixed up in the cradle. Wrong identity. Maybe I'm really a curly-headed girl!''

He threw himself on the couch.

"He's right. The design does stink. Take it off. I'm going back. Might as well get it over with. I'll bring back the material as a peace offering."

"Calvin, you can't go back there. What about Ingrid's apartment? Consider it, baby, please. Ingrid will help you. I'll help you. We'll organize your first collection. Invite everybody who's anybody. Launch you in style!"

"No—no—NO! You have to have guts to run a business. If I had guts I wouldn't be afraid of some aging fag who's got his claws into me. He owns me. He makes me less than a man—less than a woman even—less than a piece of dirt!"

The Goddess stepped down off her pedestal, the gold and white brocade fallen like a marble cloak at her feet.

"I'll make you a man," she said, certain of herself for the first time in months. Here was someone who desperately needed her, so much so he didn't realize it himself. Other men used her as a convenience, a repository, a fancy garbage can. In the past she had sometimes failed. She had challenged their manhood and forced them into hiding, into retreat from fear of castration. Calvin had nothing to lose. There was nothing she could take away from him. All she could do was give.

"Calvin," she said, sitting beside him. "Calvin, look at me."

He raised his eyes.

"Have you ever made love to a woman?" she whispered, softly, not to upset him.

"Yes . . . it was a mess. I get sick thinking about it. The dirty bitch. Remember? I told you what that dirty, rotten little bitch said . . ."

"Never mind what she said. She was a cruel, thoughtless girl. Do you remember what you did, Calvin. . . ?"

"Yes, I guess so . . . cut it out, Melissa."

"And what she did to help you? Well, this time it'll be different, Calvin. I promise you, my baby. It'll be different . . ."

She whispered directions as she guided his hands.

"You trust me, Calvin, don't you?"

(How many times had she heard those words?)

"Yes . . . Melissa?"

"What."

"You won't laugh?"

"I won't laugh. You know I won't make fun of you like that other girl. I believe in you, Calvin. I'll be gentle with you and reach for you and help you."

"Jesus Christ, I can't . . . don't make me . . ."

"Touch my arms, Calvin. Run your hands up and down my arms, slowly. Does my skin excite you? Your hands excite me. You have strong, sensitive hands. Can't you feel my pulses beating? Can't you see how my whole body is responding to you? To the

241

man in you? Waiting for your hands to go all over me?''

His eyes were squeezed shut. He could not look at what she was forcing him to do.

''Pull the slip straps down, darling. That's right. On both sides. Now, touch my breasts. Cup them in your hands . . .''

She directed traffic like a lady cop. Stop. Go. Keep right. Straight ahead. The driver was a beginner, scared stiff but willing, gaining more and more confidence as the signals became more clear.

She couldn't feel a thing. It was as if her body had been anesthetized. Yet she moaned and writhed, urging him on and on and on until his own momentum carried him to his destination and he began to believe he had been headed the right way from the start.

There was poetry in whoredom after all. This was a labor of love and compassion, the act of a drowning woman who can't save herself but tries in a burst of nobility to save someone else.

Once before she had given life only to take it back. Calvin would be reborn, sired by her, out of her. It wouldn't be as good as a baby of her own but it would be some satisfaction. Most likely he would turn on her afterwards, hating her as children bite the hands that feed them.

''Melissa,'' Calvin whispered hoarsely, his eyes still shut tight. ''Now you have to let me marry you and make you an honest woman. Right? Boy, we sure showed that bastard, didn't we, Missy? Didn't we . . ?''

# WEDNESDAY

Like many a martyr before her, Melissa felt let down. Burnt out. The way Joan of Arc might have felt the morning after if the kindling hadn't caught.

She wished Calvin had slipped away when the flames had subsided, when the last faggot had turned to ash. Now, *there* was a simile . . .

Martyrdom wasn't meant to include post-mortems. Joan of Arc didn't have to make small talk with the Dauphin about what a hot time they had had. Florence Nightingale didn't hang around during recuperation.

Flo N. Gale, shake hands with Joan of A.

*"Bon jour."*

"Howdjadoo."

Where did an American martyr go to register?

She hated to admit it, even to herself, but self-sacrifice was an ecstasy purely of the moment, something in common to both martyrs and mothers.

She pulled the sheet over her head. Martyr-in-hiding thinking evil thoughts. In retrospect, the sacrificial glory of the night before became positively distasteful.

Here she was, still on the altar, covered with a crumpled white sheet. Saint Melissa, patroness of phallic failures, protectress of a cult whose aim was to eliminate women altogether.

She was in the wrong pew.

Calvin was the last person she wanted to see. There was no first person, but Calvin was the bottom-most last. Being with him this morning would demand the same uneasy rejoicing as a reunion with some stranger you may have saved from drowning and who insists on becoming your best friend.

There was a special bond, but so what?

"Good morning, Beauty," Calvin's voice broke through the sheet barrier. "I know you're awake. I can see the sheet moving."

She peered out to see Calvin wearing Max's old bathrobe. She had appropriated it as part of the divorce spoils. There was something comforting about a man's bathrobe. A woman would never dream of buying a bathrobe four sizes too big for herself, but put her in arm's reach of a man's cavernous garment and he winds up wearing a bath towel.

Calvin was grinning at her like the honeymoon illustrations in *True Story*, a cup of coffee splashing over onto a small tray. He had filled the cup too full.

It was all too much. She hated having coffee in bed. It looked great in sheet ads or Mother's Day posters, but what could be more uncomfortable than waking up with your hair in a tangle, sleep in the corners of your eyes, a full bladder and a trayload of goodies to be first balanced and then eaten?

Melissa's first thought in the morning was to go back to sleep. Once this was overcome, she began the day with friction. Wash face with oatmeal soap and rough wash cloth. Scrub teeth with stiff-bristled brush. Do hair with hard-bristled hairbrush. Only when the body began functioning was it time for coffee.

Morning Coffee was an ambulatory beverage, to be infused with small sips at a breathless gallop, talking on the phone, painting toe-nails, sewing a bra strap. Calvin had caught her off-guard. Before she could stop him, he thrust the tray at her and left the room. She couldn't move with the awkward object in her hands. The cup wobbled on the saucer. The saucer slid from side to side threatening to career over the edge and scald her helpless flesh.

"Calvin . . ." she called, the vibrations of her voice sloshing the coffee over the tray. A few drops hit the sheet. Better not do that again. Breathing was bad enough. It jarred the tray every time she exhaled.

Where the hell *was* he? In the kitchen fixing breakfast, most likely. Well, he wouldn't find much there, unless he liked peanut butter omelets.

She couldn't move. Flat out, she balanced the tray with one hand on the ridge of sheeting over her chest. With the other hand she tried for leverage to raise herself by pressing against the mattress at her side.

It didn't work. She would have to lie here until the coffee was cool enough to spill all over her or until Calvin returned.

Next, she tried to raise her head and thrust it forward far enough to sip some of the coffee off the top of the cup. Thwarted again. The cup was so hot she couldn't touch it. Had Calvin boiled the cup with the coffee? The tray was just that bit out of reach for her aching neck muscles.

It was worse than lying on the floor with a glass of water on your forehead.

"Calvin . . ." she whispered faintly.

*Oop*. Did coffee stain?

Gingerly, she gripped the tray in her right hand and tried to lift it. Shakily and with her eyes glued to it as if it were a cobra she was defying to strike, she transferred it in a slow arc to the edge of her night table. Thinking it secure, she let go and sat up. The coffee and tray crashed to the floor, streaking the rug with liquid black.

One less item to store! Dear Max could have the rug.

"Oh, are you still here?" she asked sweetly when Calvin rushed up to see what the noise was about. It was obvious from his air of belonging that she had taken "Charity Begins At Home" far too literally. Charity should be kept as far from home as possible. The Lady of the Manor should go *out* to visit the needy. Never allow the needy to move in on her.

Oh, how she wished he would GO. There was something unhealthy about that grateful, adoring face that was driving her mad. The situation was ridiculous. She felt like a social worker about to undo a successful rehabilitation. He reminded her of the time she had helped to escort some underprivileged children to the circus and of one little boy in particular whom she overheard advising a friend to get on her good side if he wanted more than the regulation one hot dog. Never had she been so blatantly fawned upon for her favors, nor could she refuse a child so obviously in need of attention.

Now she understood why clinics were so impersonal. There was no medical word she could think of for seducing a homosexual. Maybe she could start her own movement, with a special clinic in Fire Island or Greenwich Village. Helping someone was supposed to be its own satisfaction. Why didn't the people who were helped realize that?

The most difficult part was accepting gratitude, the prolonged tedium of the aftermath. If only she could have left Calvin in a little recovery room right off the operating theater. She could have sent a faceless nurse to wake him, help him to dress and speed him on his way without having him frolic through the consulting room, trying on the doctor's coat and fooling around with the doctor's instruments.

"I thought you'd gone home," she said hopefully as he mopped up spilled coffee.

"Can't. Not until after Quentin goes to work. He doesn't leave until ten or so."

It wasn't quite nine. Another hour of Calvin was too much for a sensitive creature to contemplate so early in the morning.

She shooed him out, dressed rapidly and went downstairs. At the sight of him, she shrieked with laughter. Over Max's bathrobe, he had tied a red lace apron festooned with velvet rosebuds, a hand-wrought relic of her trousseau meant to be worn as a hostess apron far from the kitchen. He was blithely using it to protect the threadbare garment already scarred with the coffee, orange juice and make-up of six years hard wear.

"It was the only apron I could find," he explained, wiping his hands on it.

"Okay with me. You just look so funny," she said, convulsed.

247

Awkwardly, he tried to embrace her.

"Melissa . . ."

Fast footwork was an acquired instinct. She executed a reverse pivot out of his arms and picked up the frying pan he had abandoned.

"You sit down. Man works. Brings home the money. Woman stays home. Cooks the food."

"But I'm a good cook," he protested. "After we're married I'll show you. Unbelievable casseroles! Exquisite ragouts! You'll gain twenty pounds."

"I can hardly wait. Calvin, this may come as something of a shock to you but I want you to be brave. Because a woman takes a man to bed doesn't necessarily mean she wants to marry him."

This was a switch on a speech she had often heard but never thought she would be making.

"But we'd be great together! A perfect combination. With you to help me, I can be a big success. I'll buy you anything you want, when I start to make money. A Bentley—or maybe an old Rolls. A chinchilla cape for opening nights—" he wracked his brain for other wondrous gifts "—and a French poodle."

There was only one way to get through the next hour. She would have to go.

"Darling, I hate to leave you on your lonesome but I promised Ingrid to come by this morning first thing."

(She'd better call Ingrid first. No point repeating yesterday's surprise.)

Ingrid answered before the first ring stopped.

"Missy! It's you! I'm so glad! Am I in a flap. My God! I don't know what to do!"

"Be right over. In fact that's why I was calling. To say I'd be right over. Don't panic."

Nurse Kempton was on the way. Save-a-Sinner week in little old New York.

Ever practical, she carted two boxes of clothes with her in the taxi to justify spending the cab fare.

Ingrid was dressed in the paisley zip suit, only this time she was alone and obviously distraught.

"What's happened? Has Bernard pooped out? For God's sake, tell me!"

"No—it's not Bernard. It's Philip! He rang the bell at four this morning. Drunk as a lord. Knocking over milk bottles. I told him to go chase himself. I'm getting a little past night crawlers. He threatened to wake up the whole neighborhood if I didn't let him in so I did and do you know what he did? He handed me a paper ring—a Romeo y Julieta cigar band—and asked me to *marry* him! And then he got sick all over himself and when I got him cleaned up he fell asleep. I left him in the living room and locked myself in the bedroom. I kept waking up and falling back to sleep and when I peeked out at about seven-thirty, he was gone! And then just before you called, *he* called! He apologized for being drunk but he meant what he said. Now *he* wants to marry me too! I think it's just for spite!"

The law of supply and demand. You couldn't beat it.

"Wow!" was all Melissa could say.

It proved Kempton's Law of Activation. Nothing comes to her who stands and waits. Everything rushes after her who gets on her kiddie car and moves. Action begets action. Movement begets movement. Fall in love with one man, four men fall in love with you. Accept a weekend invitation to the seashore, three other people want you to sail or golf or fly to the Laurentians. It had something to do with physics, the tension of movement in one direction activating the loose strings dangling in other directions and pulling them taut.

"Too bad you're not twins," she said.

"I know. I *know*! And now I have to make up my mind, but fast. At first I thought I was dreaming last night. You've been having wacky dreams. Why not me, too? It could be catching. Then I thought, well okay, he was drunk. Men say plenty when they're drunk. But this morning—oh, this morning—he was cold sober and gentle as a lamb. He said he'd always been a confirmed bachelor, that he couldn't really see himself married but he couldn't see me getting married to somebody else so would I please marry him. Ditch Bernard and marry him. Just like that."

"Wow again. What are you going to do?"

Ingrid lay down on the couch, her face buried in the cushion, one arm dragging tragically on the floor.

Melissa paced.

"I've got an idea."

"What? What?" Ingrid rolled over and sat up, expectant.

"Let's have some coffee."

"Oh, Missy! How can you fool around at a time like this? You've got to help me think. Maybe I'll just disappear for a few days. Let both of them wait."

"That would be very dangerous. Strike when the iron is hot. And they're both red hot. You'll have to choose. Why, only a few days ago you were complaining because nobody wanted to marry you. Now, you have a choice."

"How do I make it? Put both their names in a hat and close my eyes?"

"That might be the best way. People get married for sillier reasons than that."

"But it's so *awful*. They're both so *enthusiastic*. How can I disappoint either of them?"

"If they lived in different cities, you could marry them both and commute. Three days with each and in between one day at Elizabeth Arden's to recuperate."

"They might as well live in different cities. They come from different worlds. Bernard's I can manage. Philip's frightens me. They're both so damned refined and intelligent. *Oooooooooh*! Why did I ever leave home?"

"Well, I have the infallible solution. It's the name game. We used to play it in high school to find out which boys liked us and vice versa. All you have to do is write your own name and his on a piece of paper and cross out the letters that appear in both names."

She found a piece of paper and printed

I N G R I D  G A A R D

B E R N A R D  N A H O U M

Crossing out the letters left

I G I  G D

B E A  N H O U M

"Now," Melissa continued, "you count off the letters by saying, 'Love . . . hate . . . friendship . . . marriage' and whatever word falls on the last letter shows that person's feeling for the other. According to this scientific test, you hate Bernard but—he wants to marry you!"

Ingrid smiled in spite of herself.

251

"Well, let's see how I work out with Philip!"

It was a fiasco. According to the remaining letters, she wanted to marry Philip, but he hated her.

"Clever little game," Ingrid pouted, falling back on the couch.

"Wait, what's Philip's middle name?"

"Stephen."

That was better. This time, while Ingrid Gaard felt profound friendship, Philip Stephen Winston wanted to marry her.

"Wheeeeee . . !" Ingrid twirled about the room. "I've decided. I'm going to take the veil!"

She was obviously feeling better.

"Honey, I have to go home. The Ogress—Max's mom—is due at ten and it's ten now. Keep calm and let me know what you decide."

"Okay. I'm fine now. Really. Thanks for coming."

Her eyes suddenly got that look of secret connivery that meant trouble for somebody, usually herself.

"And don't forget, Melissa. No matter what, you're moving here tomorrow. Count on it. I may still be your average neighborhood spinster. But if I am, there's plenty of room for both of us and we'll need each other on those hot summer nights. Whoever I marry—if I marry anyone—you still have to stand up for me. Promise?"

"Promise. On one condition."

"What's that?"

"I get the bouquet. This wedding bit is contagious."

(Not that there was anyone remotely eligible.)

Kip?

Married.

Dominic?

252

Morality of a jackal.

Calvin?

Suicide on a skewer.

Which left . . ?

Nobody except maybe Walter Simpson. Farfetched, too old, yet he made her think. She would skip the fact that he was married and, furthermore, she wasn't sure the two of them were speaking.

After the South American junket, she would settle down to the serious business of finding a husband. Perhaps take a job with a large banking house or a travel bureau. Some sort of decorative job. Receptionist. Customer relations, male division. The salary wouldn't matter so long as affluent gentlemen passed her way. Six months would be enough time to snare a rich, attractive specimen.

As her taxi pulled up in front of the house, she saw she was just in time. Mrs. Kempton was turning away from the door and hailing the taxi Melissa was in, thinking it empty.

"Good morning, Mrs. Kempton. It's me. Sorry if I kept you waiting."

Why hadn't Calvin let her in? He must have gone.

The older woman greeted her coldly.

"Your young—companion—came to the door, Melissa. I didn't think it seemly to wait. There's no need to be so brazen about your behavior. Other folks aren't quite as sophisticated as you."

"Now, Mrs. Kempton," Melissa was fumbling for her key determined to grin no matter what the old idiot said. "That's just a young neighbor of mine who came to help me pack. I had an errand and asked him to wait. He's very sweet. You'll adore him. He designs dresses.''

She had half a mind to add, ''And he's a social homosexual, too, which I've been trying to cure as my community service project,'' except that Mrs. Kempton would probably pretend she didn't know what a homosexual was.

''I do think you might have had the good manners not to flaunt your indiscretions at me quite so . . . openly. I *am* Max's mother, after all.''

(As if she didn't know.) The damned key was acting up again. Thank God she was moving. No more struggling for supremacy over this key.

The older woman was at her elbow, breathing down her neck.

''What's the matter? Can't you make it work?''

''I can mind my own business and keep my mouth shut!'' she answered, angrier at the door than her friendly adviser. Better ring for Calvin. She had wanted to avoid introducing them. Now it was inevitable. She hoped Calvin wouldn't be kittenish.

Mrs. Kempton stepped back, visibly shaken. ''You're a rude, disrespectful chit,'' she said. ''I won't soil myself by going inside. Max will have to do without the furniture. Rather than take anything from you, I'd rather . . .''

''Watch out, Mrs. Kempton! The grate! It's loose!''

She was too late. The older woman stepped backward onto the loose edge of the grate, catching her heel in a rung. Her weight tipped the grating up at the far end, pulling her down with it as the near side slid into the declivity. She crumpled flat as a house of cards or a balloon pricked with a pin. A hatpin! God in Heaven. The hatpin!

As she fell, the side of her face hit the sidewalk with a sickening crunch, knocking off her hat. She lay unconscious, her legs twisted beneath her, her face a deathly gray, her mouth open and slack, her hat fallen rakishly over one open eye.

Calvin had opened the door and laugher nervously. A woman in slacks stopped to help.

"Whatever you do," she told Melissa firmly, "don't touch her! Young man, go in and call the police. Get an ambulance. What happened?"

"She's dead!" Melissa whimpered. "And I killed her!"

"Keep calm," the woman ordered. "I'll watch her. Now go in and get a blanket or a coat. It's warm out but she may be suffering from shock. I once took a first aid course. You have to keep them warm."

She stooped beside the lifeless form.

"She's not dead. She's breathing all right so get a move on. Her heart's beating and there's breath coming out of her mouth."

Calvin came out with a coat. "Who is she, Missy? She rang the bell and when I answered she asked were you in and I said you'd be right back and she couldn't wait."

"She's my late mother-in-law. Oh, God, I mean my *ex*-mother-in-law. My *former* mother-in-law. Max's mother. I better call Max. She's dead and I killed her!"

His secretary found him making a speech at a sales meeting. He was on the way.

Melissa suddenly snapped to. Taking her bathroom

sponge and the pillow off her bed, she gently raised the woman's head and wiped away the blood and concrete fragments. Now, after the first shock, she felt oddly calm and in control. A few people stood at a respectful distance watching but she ignored them. She sent Calvin back for a fresh pillow case. Everything had to be as clean as possible. Together, they eased the clean pillow under the waxen head.

The police car and ambulance arrived simultaneously, Max a moment later.

"What happened, Melissa?" He was deadly calm, too. There was something about emergencies that brought out the stiff upper lip in people.

"It was all my fault, Max. We were arguing and she stepped back on the grate. It was loose and she fell."

"But what were you doing outside?"

"I had to go over to Ingrid's this morning and I got back just as she arrived . . . Oh, Max . . . what can I say?"

The doctor who had motioned Max to stay back was easing the crumpled form into normal position.

"We didn't move her, doctor," Melissa said in a strained voice. "I just bathed her face. We didn't move her." It seemed to important to have obeyed the rules. "I know you're not supposed to move people."

Max held her arm. "It's all right, Melissa. The doctor knows what he's doing."

The young man in the white jacket spoke as he worked. "You were right. The best thing a bystander can do is keep the victim warm. I don't find anything broken in either extremities but I'm afraid the skull may be fractured. That was a bad wallop on the side

256

of her head. I've stopped the bleeding temporarily. But she's in shock. I think we'd better rush her to Bellevue. Are either of you next of kin?''

"Yes. I'm her son," Max said as another car, with MD license plates, pulled up to the curb.

"Good. It's Dr. Sheldon." Max went to meet him. "I had my secretary call him."

The general practicioner hurried to the patient's side.

"It's a good thing this ambulance is here," he said after a quick examination. "We'll take her straight to Bellevue, transfer her to my hospital later on."

Max started to protest.

"Don't worry. If we wait for a private ambulance, we could be in trouble. The municipal ambulance is here. I'll ride with her, see that she's comfortable. My young colleague has taken care of the preliminaries. You stay here with Melissa. You both look wobbly. Take a brandy or other alcoholic stimulant. I'll telephone you from the hospital once I know what's what."

He smiled reassuringly.

"She's a tough old lady. I can tell from the way she's hanging onto her pocketbook, unconscious or not."

Max held Melissa against his side, his arm around her shoulder, as the two doctors and attendants carefully slid his mother onto a stretcher and into the ambulance.

"I think I should ride along with you."

"No," his doctor said firmly. "Too many relatives ride in ambulances. She's unconscious. You can't help

257

her. Take care of Melissa—and yourself. There's nothing you can do except make yourself miserable."

He closed the ambulance doors, only to open them again. "There *is* something you can do. Get somebody to throw a dime in the parking meter next to my car or I'll have to add a five dollar ticket to your bill." He grinned impishly. "Now, don't worry, Max. She's in competent hands."

Calvin touched Melissa's arm deferentially. She had forgotten him completely, that he was there, that he was even alive.

"Guess I'd better go," he said. "I'm just in the way. If you need me for anything call."

She nodded, unhearing.

"I've sent a man to get a board to put over that grate," the police officer said. "Meantime, we'll leave a red flag to keep people away. I'm sorry to have to trouble you at a time like this but there are a few questions I have to ask to fill in my report."

"Come inside, officer," said Max. "I think we'll all feel better sitting down."

Melissa hadn't realized how shaky her knees were until she tried to walk.

The officer pulled out an orange form and began to ask monotonous questions of officialdom.

Date. Name. Sex. Age.

Max gave the answers. Melissa answered them in her mind.

Date? The day before eviction, the day before Ingrid's wedding, the day of Calvin's salvation, the day Melissa got even.

Name? Widow, Mother. Mother-in-law. Voodoo victim. Bitch no matter what.

258

Sex? Dirty, dirty, dirty word. Immaculate deception. Female, yes. Woman, no.

Age? She was surprised to hear 54. Young for having a son of 35. Too young to die.

"Were either of you witnesses to the accident?"

"I—I was," Melissa said brokenly. "It was all my fault . . ."

"My wife is very upset, officer. She and mother didn't get along too well. You know how it is . . ."

"Yeah, don't tell me. I have a mother-in-law myself . . ."

"My mother met my wife in the street. She was waiting for her to open the door and unfortunately stepped on the grating. My wife feels at fault because the grate has been loose for some time but she did nothing about fixing it because the house has been bought by real estate promoters and she has been forced to move—tomorrow, in fact."

"She?" the officer said, questioningly.

"Yes. We're divorced, you see. This is my wife's home."

"Ah, a nice friendly divorce. Well, that does it. No foul play. Victim taken to Bellevue. Next of kin approved. Thank you, Mr.—Kempton."

Calvin walked home in a state of elation. Accidents were very thrilling. This was the first one in which he had known someone. Police. Ambulances. Doctors. Crowds. It was wonderful. He had rarely felt so exhilarated, so close to life and stark realism. That young ambulance doctor with his crew haircut and white sneakers. The copper with the billy stick and the pistol. Public servants, all ready and willing to serve him in event of an emergency. He wondered how it felt to be lying on a sidewalk, unable to move, staring up into the sympathetic eyes of strangers, submitting to the strong ministrations of a strange doctor, being carried on a stretcher to an ambulance and transported at high speed through the city streets, the bell clanging and everyone having to jump out of the way for you!

So that was Max. Melissa hadn't introduced them. You couldn't exactly blame her. What with the accident and all she was pretty upset. She probably pushed the old lady. Served the old bag right for picking on her. He was glad Max had come. Otherwise he would have had to stay and comfort Melissa. He didn't like comforting people. All that slobbering and Be-a-Brave-Little-Person. His kindergarten teacher had always said, "Be a brave little person," when someone shoved a tack in your arm or pushed you in the sandbox in your new pants that weren't supposed to get dirty.

This was one of those times when Calvin worried about his reactions. Here was this old lady out cold on the sidewalk, twisted up like a pretzel, maybe dying. He just couldn't work up a sweat over it. He knew he should feel compassion or sorrow but he couldn't. He was glad to get away because he was sure his feelings would show. He wouldn't have been able to look sad for long. He might have started whistling or kidding around with Melissa.

During the night he had thought maybe Melissa really would marry him. But he had to admit now that he really didn't think she would. Why the hell should she? Who was he? He was Calvin, formerly mouse, formerly ass-kisser to His Majesty Quentin the Unquenchable. That was a good one.

By now the apartment would be empty. He would steal everything he could carry, sell it and move into the Y until Melissa got straightened out and he could move into Ingrid's apartment.

Quentin wouldn't dare file a complaint against him. His sense of public relations wouldn't let him. Nor would his pride. To have it known that somebody walked out on him? Cleaned him out of shirts and portable antiques? He would never admit to that. His story would be he threw Calvin out and gave him everything to pay him off. It was too bad he couldn't figure a way to kidnap the Senegalese boy. He was Quentin's most precious possession, the portrait running a close second. If he thought he could get something for it, he would take the portrait, but who would buy such a monstrosity? Instead, he had a better idea.

The apartment was quiet. The air close.

"That bitch never did learn to open a window," he muttered to himself, drawing back the heavy gold drapes and opening the air vents.

Suddenly hungry, he wondered if Quentin had bought some more croissants.

He made his way toward the kitchen at the other end of the apartment. In the brick-lined room, he noted the antique gun restored to its place. In the red velvet bedroom, the air grew stuffier.

"The bastard. It's like sleeping in a coffin. He thinks air is poison."

The portieres of the four-poster bed were closed. Maybe, after breakfast, he would take a little nap before clearing out. There was plenty of time. It had been quite a night. He had kept himself awake to avoid making any mistakes.

He started to pull back the bed curtain but suddenly remembered his earlier idea. The portrait. He must leave Quentin an extra-special farewell note.

Finding a bottle of ketchup, he returned to the reception room and squirted the thick red sauce all over the portrait's delicate white shirtfront. Pleased with his artistry, he carried the empty bottle to the kitchen and ate all that was in the refrigerator, which was two ripe plums.

Yawning now, he returned to the bedroom and pulled the ornate cord. Quentin lay before him, on his back, arms reaching up in grotesque welcome, face contorted in painful ecstacy, mouth open and seeming about to speak through blue lips. He was wearing his matador costume complete to the white silk hose and pink velvet shoes.

A note beside him, written in white ink on the fuschia letter paper that he affected as a trademark, said, "I know you'll be back but it will be too late. It is six o'clock in the morning. The eastern sky is a pomegranate sunburst. I know she has won and I have lost you forever. I have tried to keep you happy with me. I have lost. This is the only way to prove my love." It was signed with the beautiful gothic Q which Quentin had learned to write through diligent practice.

Calvin closed the portieres and stuffed the note in his pocket. He wasn't sleepy now. There was too much to do. Opening the cupboard, he pulled out all the suit cases and began to fill them. He would work his way carefully from room to room, picking and choosing only the smallest, most valuable mementoes of his friendship with Quentin. The daily cleaning woman didn't come until two. He would have plenty of time.

Dr. Sheldon called to tell Max he should not come to the hospital until evening visiting hours. His mother was under heavy sedation and could have no visitors until then. Time would tell. She was in serious condition but the hospital was only minutes away by taxi. There was no point sitting in a dreary waiting room for hours. They were taking X-rays now. Preliminary examination had shown no internal injuries or broken bones.

The police had gone. A little red flag fluttered outside the window as if it were a skating rink. It was not yet noon on her last day in this house, Melissa realized, and here she was alone with the man who had first brought her here and whose mother was dying or already dead.

"Is she dead, Max?" she demanded when he hung up the phone. "I can stand it. Tell me if she's dead."

"She's not dead, Missy. Calm yourself. She's in serious condition but she's very much alive."

"Max . . . you don't understand. I have to tell you this. It was all my fault. I tried to kill her. I—I didn't touch her but I *willed* it to happen. I wanted her dead!"

"You keep saying that and you've got to stop. You're not responsible. You're suffering from shock. Come on now. Put your feet up and try and take it easy."

"No—no—NO," she protested, stamping her foot. "You must listen to me." Haltingly, she told him about the voodoo session with Ingrid, how she got carried away and thrust the hatpin again and again into the figure of his mother. "It started out as a silly joke but you can see what a joke it is. Everyone's been

263

warning me to fix that grate, including my own mother, but I wouldn't. I didn't. I've been waiting for your mother to come here so I could kill her on it. Oh, God, what if she dies, Max. How can you look at me? I'm a murderess."

He held her at arm's length, looking her full in the eyes. It was the first time in many months that they had truly looked at each other.

"If my mother dies it will be because of an accident, Melissa. Do you hear me? An *accident*! If anyone is responsible, I'm the one. She was nervous and a little frightened this morning, and that's probably why she didn't notice the grate and why she fell. People have accidents when they're upset. And she was upset this morning because I upset her yesterday afternoon. She couldn't sleep last night. I heard her prowling around. I told her everything, Melissa . . ."

"About the—baby?"

"Yes," he said. "I thought it was about time she shared the failure of our marriage. I didn't realize how hard she would take it. So you see, we can each blame ourselves for what's happened or we can leave the burden of blame with her. Or we can forget about blame and pray for her recovery. All three of us have committed a terrible injustice against ourselves and each other and I think we've all punished ourselves quite enough."

"Oh, Max," she cried, "I'm so confused. So much has happened this morning and tomorrow the movers and Ingrid getting married—unless she doesn't of course—and I still have to cancel the phone service and take care of all the other details—and meantime that poor woman is lying unconscious in Bellevue

Hospital and there's nothing we can do. Anyway, don't think you have to stay here with me. I'm okay. You have meetings and things. You can go, Max. I'll be all right.''

''Melissa, I told my mother something else. I told her I was still in love with you and wanted you back if you would come back.''

''Max, you're saying that because you think it'll make me feel better. You wouldn't want me back. Now now. We'd have too much to forget. I don't know how to build something. I can only destroy.''

He pulled her forward and held her against the length of his body. After a moment, he kissed her forehead.

''Melissa,'' he whispered in her hair, ''you wanted a baby. I made you get rid of it. It was so foolish, so unnecessary, so adolescent. Well, I want to make retribution. After four years. You're going to have that baby, Melissa, because I'm giving it back to you—if you'll still have my baby.''

Tears choked her voice. ''You're crazy, Max. After what's happened? A baby?''

''We've come full circle,'' he said wryly. ''This is where we began. Once you accused me of not being able to impregnate you after we were married, that I could only do it when we weren't married. You rubbed my face in the mud with it. Well, we aren't married now. This house has a God-like quality. It exercises omnipotent power. It gave us a baby once. Maybe it can give us another child before we leave it forever.''

''Maybe you're right,'' she said snappishly, trying to regain the sarcastic tone she used as defense against Max. ''You've always thought sex was dirty. Maybe now I'm dirty enough for you. I've slept with so many

265

different men this past year I've lost count and today I tried to kill your mother.''

She broke down, crying uncontrollably. As the spasms subsided, she found Max watching her, sober-faced, quiet, waiting.

Drained of tears and guilt and hatred, she allowed him to take her hand and lead her up the stairs he had been afraid to ascend a few days before. They climbed over the battered suitcases, mottled trunks and boxes tied with colored string that littered the landing and bedroom, the debris of wanton sexuality.

Soon she was aware of the phone ringing. Ringing, ringing, ringing. But the phone was ringing in the present and they had returned to the past. Re-living the past to regain the present. The ringing grew louder and more insistent until gradually her entire body vibrated with the sound. Somewhere in the swelling intensity might be the seed. Was what was past past?

When the plangent beat had subsided to a low hum, she arose and groped about the room for something to cover her suddenly unbearable nakedness. She wanted something feminine and adorable but everything was packed. All she could find was the battered old bathrobe.

Max wrapped her up in it and carried her to the chaise where she lay curled up in his lap, her arms around his neck. There were all kinds of products on the market for erasing the wear and tear of time, for covering up shabbiness and mistakes with bright, new colors. They could not erase or cover up four years' decay, so they would have to abandon it. Move away and leave it. She feel asleep.

She awoke to the familiar clamor of the telephone.

She was on her bed. Max had gone but a note said he was taking some clothes down to the hospital.

It was Service calling. As usual, come flood or famine or the hydrogen bomb, nothing stopped Groupsville from checking in.

Dominic had obviously forgotten his slight and would meet her at Michael's at ten. Bert Barkas was off to Europe and wanted some addresses. Ingrid had called four times, the last to say she and Philip could not wait another instant for her. They were off to Greenwich to get married this afternoon and then to New England for a quiet honeymoon. The operator read the message in a bored voice. Ingrid was happy, happy, happy. The key was under the mat.

Poor Bernard. She wondered how Ingrid had told him or whether she had told him at all. It wasn't so much cowardice as the practical matter of hanging on to all possibilities in case first choice conked out. If Philip changed his mind, or got a flat tire, or forgot his birth certificate . . . she had an alternate groom. Ingrid never took anything for granted until it was an accomplished fact.

Poor Bernard. She wondered what he would do. Fly to Haiti alone? Have dinner with his mother?

She asked the Service operator to do a few things for her. To call Kip and say she would be unable to make South America, and Dominic to say she would be unable to make Michael's. She made a note to call Bert Barkas. European addresses were something she had lots of.

Finally, she thanked the operator for her kindness in the past. She was discontinuing the service, she

267

said, because she was getting married and would have no further need of its narcosis.

"Well," said the operator philosophically, "you sure had it good while it lasted. Good luck and you don't know what you're letting yourself in for. I've been married twelve years and nobody with a sexy English accent wants to meet me anywhere. Believe me, it can make you think."

# THURSDAY MORNING

They would have to hurry. Dr. Sheldon had promised a ten minute visit at noon. As it turned out, no visitors had been permitted the night before. Mrs. Kempton was conscious now and resting comfortably, as they say in hospitalese. With care and no complications, she would be out of bed in a week.

The big van had arrived early. Max was supervising the delicate business of moving furniture across fifteen feet of pavement without smashing it to bits. It was unutterably wonderful to have a man in charge. Melissa had found by experience that the "helpless lone female" was effective in some situations but only when the opponent was in the mood to be a knight in shining armor. Otherwise, a helpless girl got just what you might expect. Short shrift. A strong, forceful no-nonsense man left no doubt as to what was expected.

Walter arrived with two workmen in tow. He apologized to Melissa for not calling. He had heard about the accident late in the afternoon.

"The grating is the new owner's responsibility,"

he said. "I checked into it this morning. They're fully insured. Mrs. Kempton must be sure to enter a claim. I have some other news for you, Melissa, though I'm not sure whether you'll be interested."

"This is my husband, Max Kempton," she said. The two men had been staring at each other.

"How do you do? Well," this was hardly the moment for the story of his forthcoming divorce, "the decision has been made to pull the house down."

She and Max turned to look at it.

"That's progress. It's passed its usefulness," Max said. "Like a bad tooth, extraction is better than lingering decay."

"Oh, how you talk!" She laughed wholeheartedly at his pompous try for profundity.

The workmen were nailing together a heavy wooden cover to fit over the grating to prevent further accidents. When the last of the furniture had been stuffed into the van, she and Max made a final tour of the house. Empty, it was already a strange place. Standing on the floor in the far corner of the living room was the ceramic figurine. She had not wrapped it in newspaper with the other bits and pieces. She had planned to leave it behind.

Now she picked it up.

"I'm going to smash it into a million pieces," she said vehemently. "I never want to see it again."

"No—don't."

Max took it from her.

"It's crude, darling, but it has great feeling. I think that's why I hated it. Because you could give such passion to a piece of clay but not to me. But I've changed my mind. Let's take it with us. It's a Mother

270

Figure all right and if I can help it, you're going to look like this three or four more times before we're through.''

"Then come on, Max!" she said exultantly. "We've got everything. Let's go!"

She ran to the door and flung it open. The key. She suddenly remembered the key.

"Walter," she called. "I have a present for you. A masculine key."

He grinned sadly as she held it out.

"No, I've got a better idea," she said, going over to the grating which in another moment would be shielded from sight.

"Gentlemen, excuse me," she said, stepping nimbly over the tools and slats of wood.

Straddling the grate, she dropped the keys between her feet. The delayed plop reminded her of the time she lost her sunglasses in the w.c. of a French farmhouse.

When she stepped back, the workmen lifted the wooden cover and fitted it into place.

"We're ready, darling," Max called as the van prepared to leave.

She turned toward him, begging him with her entire will to be her sun, source of her energy and life itself. Halfway across the pavement she stopped. The telephone was ringing.

"Don't answer it!" Max cried savagely, seizing her arm.

Once . . . twice . . . if she didn't answer, whoever it was might hang up.

"I have to, Max! I have to know who it is!" She tore free and raced through the open door, into the living room, snatching the phone from its cradle after the third ring. She could see Max staring at her through the window and turned her back.

"Hello?"

It was Kip.

"I was about to call you when I got your message," he said calmly. "The plans have been changed. We don't leave for Caracas next Tuesday—"

"Oh, but Kip—"

"We leave tonight—10:50 out of Idlewild. This gives you the whole day to get ready—only one suit-case, *please*, darling, I hate to pay for overweight unless it's camera equipment—I'll meet you at Michael's at seven."

"Kip! Please shut up! I'm not going with you. I sent you a message!" Dammit! What good was having a service if it didn't do all the cowardly things like cancel a dentist appointment or break off a love affair?

"Yes, your service delivered it. What's happened? Have you had a btter offer?"

"A better offer!" She could have killed him but then she laughed. "In a way, yes, Kip. I've decided to go back to Max. My ex-husband, remember? He's waiting for me outside."

"There is a middle-European proverb about warmed-over stew," Kip replied tersely. "You're not cut out to be an ordinary wife, Melissa. You are your own woman! Don't think he's going to take care of you. Nobody can take care of anybody. We all must look after ourselves, and ourselves alone. That is the first natural law."

"Then why should I come with you, Kip?" she

272

asked, her neck tight, her back taut, the pressure of Max's eyes upon her.

"Because I am taking you to South America and you have never been to South America. Because I am going to photograph you for a big magazine and you have never appeared in a magazine. Because I am nice to you in bed and because I offer you pure romance and pure adventure. I will fill your eyes and your mind and your body with colors, sights and sensations you have never experienced before."

"I'm sorry, Kip. I can't just live from adventure to adventure. I can't spend my life on a roller coaster."

"That is your mistake. Life *is* a roller coaster. If you slow down, you fall off."

"Max is waiting, Kip. I have to go. Enjoy your trip. And don't worry, you won't have trouble finding another girl."

"Think over what I said, Melissa," he said quickly. "I'll be waiting for you at Michael's—at seven sharp. Don't be late, my lovely."

He hung up.

Melissa smiled wanly at Max and reached for his hand as a workman splashed the first whitewash "X" on the bedroom window. Regret, anger and a hollow sense of loss filled her eyes and dampened her palms. If there were an embryo churning away inside her, she wouldn't know for sure for at least four weeks. It would be pointless to marry Max again unless she were sure, wouldn't it? After all, Max himself admitted that he couldn't knock her up when they were married.

Her passport was in order, as always. She had all day to decide about Kip. Meanwhile, why commit herself so completely to Max, why sell out her free-dom, her independence, her personal identity by mov-ing into his apartment? What was the big hurry? Besides, she wasn't totally homeless. She had some-where to go. A certain key lay under a certain mat.

"Max," she said, staring out of the taxi window, her back turned to him. "I think you'd better drop me at Ingrid's, darling. Most of my clothes are there—I've been taking them over in batches—and, well, I prom-ised Ingrid I'd water her plants."

She could feel his disbelief but she could not turn to face him.

"Give the driver the address," he said, after a few hollow minutes.

She stayed frozen in her uncomfortable position until the cab pulled up in front of Ingrid's house. Max did not get out to help her. She stood on the sidewalk and reached into the back seat for her makeup case.

"I'll call you later, Max," she said, lightly. "Have a good day at the office."

Brutally, he yanked her arm, pulled her forward with bruising force across the floor of the taxi.

"You're committing suicide, Melissa!" he cried, his voice like the skirl of a dying bag-pipe. "You're throwing yourself away. You're dead! Dead!"

Pressing into her breasts and ribs were the metal backrests of the jump seats that folded into the floor. As Max loosened his grip on her arm, she slowly pulled herself upright.

"You're wrong, Max," she said quietly, closing the taxi door between them. "I'm alive. It's the only way I know how to live."

The telephone.

"*Don't* answer," he said.

"Yes."

"It might be *Ingrid*."

"Yes."

"Wouldn't *she* be surprised?"

"Yes."

"I mean about me getting in from *Paris* this morning and everything?"

"Yes."

"—And calling *her* up and finding you?"

"Yes."

"Things certainly happen *fast* in New York."

"Yes."

At seven she had gone to Michael's and found a note from Kip. There's been a shift in assignments. He was off to Beirut. If he didn't get killed, he would send her a plane ticket to meet him in Pamplona July 10th for the bull festival. Bull was right. A breath-holder first class.

Poor Kip. Where once he romped through beginnings, middles and ends of romance, now he had only heart enough for romantic gestures. Worse, where once he fled before dawn, now he fled before dusk.

Poor Max, too. She had called him, but the doleful switchboard girl said there'd been an emergency call from the hospital.

And, finally, poor Calvin. She had called him, but a stranger's voice said Quentin was dead, Calvin gone.

This man was certainly right. Things certainly happened fast in New York.

"You ever been to Paris, *cher-ry*?"

"Yes."

"God*dam!*"             he             crowed,
"—you . . . me . . . Ingrid . . . Paris,
France . . . New York, New York . . . it's a *small*
world!"
"Yes."

# EPILOGUE

Sitting cross-legged on the floor, her face wet with tears, Stephanie looked beseechingly at Ingrid. "And was she pregnant?"

Ingrid smiled. "She was."

"With—*me*?"

"Yes, you nitwit."

"You mean—" She was thrilled by the idea. "I was conceived out of wedlock?"

"You're what used to be called a love child."

"Oh—" The younger woman's face clouded.

"What?"

"She and Daddy *had* to get married again. Because of me."

"That's not so. Max courted your mother all over again. He didn't know she was pregnant. She really didn't know for sure for close to six weeks. And she certainly didn't tell him. In fact, the reason she agreed to marry him again was *because* he didn't know you were on the way. He convinced her he had changed and things would be different and they would be happy.''

''So why weren't they?''

''They tried, Stephanie. They tried for twelve years, as you know—''

''Why'd she have to do it? Why couldn't she be like other mothers?''

''No mothers are like other mothers. Mothering is a myth perpetrated by the media.''

''But—'' Stephanie choked up. The memory of Melissa's defection hurt her as deeply now as it had half her own lifetime ago. ''—for a *trumpet* player?''

''Stephanie—''

''I'm sorry, Aunt Ingrid. I can't accept what she did.''

''Try to understand—''

''I can't understand. I didn't understand then and I can't understand now. How could she leave us for—''

''It was something she had to do.''

''She left me for—a roll in the hay.''

Ingrid smiled. ''There are worse reasons for leaving.''

''I expected—''

''You expected too much from her. She expected too much from Max. Max expected her to forget her romantic nature. She expected him to be different. That's the trouble with all of us. We all expect too much. And now I'm expecting *you* to forget your hurt and feelings of rejection and to understand your mother.''

''Well, she expected us to forgive her!'' Stephanie said belligerently.

''So—was that too much to ask?''

"She wanted us to forget the whole thing and pretend like it never happened."

"And why couldn't you do that?"

"Well, Daddy—"

"Don't go blaming it on Max. Max wanted her back. He told me. It was you, Stephanie. You who refused to talk to her, made her feel like dirt. I sat in that living room and watched you sit on the arm of your father's chair. 'I'll take care of you, Daddy. We don't need her!' "

Stephanie stood up and ran a brush through her hair. "You've always been on her side. I came here because I thought you were my friend."

"I'm your friend and your godmother. I love you and I want you to be happy."

"Can't you at least admit my mother wrecked my life?"

Melissa stood in the doorway as if by magic. "*My* mother wrecked *my* life. *Your* mother wrecked *your* life and undoubtedly *you* will wreck *your* child's life."

Behind her, Max Kempton said wryly, "I'll leave *my* mother out of this one, if you don't mind."

The newcomers stood hesitantly, unsure of their welcome.

"For God's sake, come on in," Ingrid embraced them. "We were just talking about you."

"Stephanie—" Melissa addressed her daughter. It was the first time they had seen each other in two years. Stephanie had declined to invite her mother to the wedding.

"What are you doing here! Daddy—" the angry young woman turned her wrath on her father. "Why did you bring her?"

279

"I didn't bring her, she brought me," Max explained.

"Tom came to see me," Melissa said.

"How *could* he? It's none of your business."

Melissa lit a cigarette, sipped the Campari and soda Ingrid gave her and replied, "*You* are my business. Whether you like it or not. I'm your mother and that's why I'm here and that's why Max is here."

"And where's Tom? Hiding in the hall?" Stephanie sneered.

"He's not *hiding* anywhere. He's waiting downstairs in the lobby."

"Sure—and what's he waiting for? For me to say he's perfect and I'm the miserable bitch and he's right and I'm wrong?"

"He's waiting to tell you he loves you, Steph," Max assured her.

"Oh, sure—"

"Yes, sure," Melissa said. "The three of us just had lunch and—"

"Oh, great—you're fine ones to patch up *our* marriage."

"We're the only ones," Max countered. "Who else, if not us?"

Stephanie looked from one to the other. "I haven't seen the two of you together in a long time."

"Too long a time," Ingrid put in.

Everyone in the room suddenly became aware of the fact that Melissa and Max were looking at their own reflection in Ingrid's ormolu mirror, each holding the other's eyes and smiling.

Without too much conviction, Stephanie complained, "What's Tom doing downstairs? I suppose he blamed everything on me?"

"He doesn't blame anybody. Not even himself."

"I'd better go to him. How *could* you leave him sitting downstairs all by himself?" she accused both her parents with a single stabbing finger before rushing from the room.

"Don't blame me," Max half sang, slipping his arm through Melissa's.

"For falling in love with you," Melissa half-sang in response.

The last thing Ingrid saw as she slipped from the room was the reflection in her mirror of a man and woman poised on the edge of an embrace.

## LESLIE
Dorothy Taylor

**LB566TK $1.95**
Contemporary Romance

For Leslie McAllister, life had not been good. Not until she met Andrew Phillips. Then things started to go her way, and for the first time she could look to the future without dread. But the return of her husband changed all that, and she was forced into a perilous charade!

## LOVE'S GOLDEN CIRCLE
Margaret Maitland

**LB557TK $1.95**
Novel

Set amid the passions and mysteries of ancient Egypt, Margaret Maitland's latest bestseller floods onto the territory prepared by DAWN OF DESIRE. How could the Queen of Egypt reconcile her love for a foreign prince with her duty to her brother and her country? With the power of the Nile itself, the story of Queen Cornelia's love for Prince Kenkenes will sweep readers along—a story so great only a goddess could live it! This cover will be foiled.

## CATERINA
Eveline Amstutz

**LB575RK $2.25**
Novel

Bride for a year, widow for a lifetime, Caterina drew strength from her tragedy and became the rock on which a dynasty would be built. Through the tragedy and turmoil of four generations, La Marchesa Caterina was the force that made her family survive!

## DISCO
Chelsea Farraday

**LB599TK $1.95**
Novel

What's the story behind the hottest disco in New York, Michelle's? It's the story of Michelle herself, from her days as a singer in a New Orleans whorehouse to her affair with the Mafia don who gave her the disco.

## PASSION'S THIEF
**Louise MacKendrick**

LB573TK   $1.95
Novel

She was a woman alone against her powerful cousin
and his allies, but Denise de Chabionniere found
friends to stand by her—in the slums and gutters of
Paris! With the help of her beloved Lyle, the army of
beggars would carry her struggle into the halls of the
Louvre!

## BY LOVE DIVIDED
**Rebecca Burton**

LB558TK   $1.95
Novel

The Battle of Britain. The Nazis rained death and
terror from the skies every night. A child is left alone,
his mother dead; his father in the air fighting the
Luftwaffe. The quiet heroism of the child's nurse
matches his father's and the two adults are drawn
together. Somewhere, in the rubble, love will find a
space to grow—and so will sales. This cover will be
foiled.

## PAIRING OFF
**Julian Moynahan**

LB642   $1.75
Novel

Selected by *The New York Times* as "one of the year's
best," this rollicking, bawdy romance is reminiscent
of J. P. Donleavy at his best. ". . . a unified, moving,
continually entertaining masterpiece. . . ."—*The
Los Angeles Times*. "PAIRING OFF is an Irish
happening."—*Time* Magazine.
Setting: Boston, MA and Ireland, 1950's

## INTIMATE STRANGERS
**Chelsea Farraday**

LB608   $1.95
Novel

They were three women at the same place at the same
time with the same dream—or so they thought. Jes-
sica found only the emptiness of glamour and pres-
tige, Sally found the unhappiness of a loveless marriage, and only Evvie found the career they had all
sought—at the cost of her private life.

## TWICE DEAD
**Larry D. Names**

LB601KK $1.75
Novel

Did Lee Harvey Oswald die in 1959? Reporter Tom Regan finds evidence that this may be the case, and he follows the lead on a trail that takes him to the core of the conspiracy to assassinate President Kennedy—and to the brink of death!

## THE PRO
**Bob Packard**

LB647 $2.25
Novel

Golf was more than a game to Doug Austin—it was the way to get off the assembly line, the way to get rich, the way to get away from his wife, and the way to win glamorous Melinda Long. But for Doug Austin, the high life only meant he had a long way to fall! Setting: Pennsylvania, Las Vegas, the pro golf tour, contemporary.

## MILLIE & CLEVE
**Jess Carr**

LB615 $2.25
Novel

Prohibition hadn't changed anything in the hills— moonshiners and the law still kept up a fast-paced competition. Cleve was a deputy sheriff who wanted to be the best sheriff Edison County ever saw, but he was in love with Millie—and she and her father were already at the top of the moonshiners' heap! Setting: Southern United States, 1920's

## PROMISE ME ROMANCE
**Jeannie Sakol**

LB607 $1.95
Novel

A public relations agency on the verge of success in London, a variety of wealthy and handsome lovers— Margaret Sturtevant had everything a modern woman wants, but all she really wanted was a chance to give it all up and be a housewife for the man she loved!

## THE QUEEN'S RIVAL
**Shannon Clare**

**LB590TK $1.95**
**Historical Romance**

In Victorian England, nothing was more important than propriety, and the Queen's family set the example. But Alexandra de Grey, separated from the husband who murdered her brother, was drawn by passion into an affair that threatened the stability of the Empire—with the Queen's husband!

## POWER OF DARKNESS
**Doris Sutcliffe Adams**

**LB567TK $1.95**
**Historical Romance**

Durande was alone against the forces of evil until Helie returned from the Crusades to stand by her side. Two against the demon horde was still unequal, but the young couple found a love that gave them the strength they needed to prevail.

## FORBIDDEN SPLENDOR
**Ralph Hayes**

**LB565TK $1.95**
**Historical Romance**

General Bonaparte's army could defeat the Egyptians, but who would fight his battles with the faithless Josephine? His only ally was Pauline Foures unhappily married to an officer in the French army. Their flirtation grew into a passion so fiery that it could consume an empire yet unborn!

## BANNERS OF DESIRE
**Lorinda Hagen**

**LB598RK $2.25**
**Historical Romance**

As an actress, Caroline travelled both sides of the lines in the Civil War, and as a spy she played both sides as well. Finally, she had to decide between her family and duty in the South, and her heart and future in the North!

## DAUGHTER OF CONQUEST    LB646   $2.25
**Robert E. Mills**    **Historical Romance**

Isolated within the French colony in Cairo, Louise Rouland longed for an adventure to relieve her boredom. Martin Braddock, an American engineer, joined Napoleon's expedition to Egypt to have a part in history. When they met they knew their fates were one, but adventure, history, and Napoleon's ambition stood between them!

## THIS SPLENDID LAND    LB638   $1.95
**Chet Cunningham**    **Historical Romance**

The Breckenridge Saga concludes with Jed and Jeannie building their new ranch in Texas into an empire. As the ranch grows, so do the passions of those on it, and Jed's tempestuous affair with the Mexican beauty Teresa leads to an armed showdown, with the whole future at stake!
Setting: Texas Panhandle, 1840's

## DESTINY AND DESIRE    LB639   $1.95
**Lorinda Hagen**    **Historical Romance**

Orphaned Letitia Cooper got a sudden opportunity—to go west and live on her uncle's ranch. Before long, he'd been killed, and someone was out to get control of the Sierra Lorena spread. Two men stood at Letty's side, but one of them wanted to kill her!
Setting: Nevada, 1867

**SEND TO: LEISURE BOOKS**
            P.O. Box 270
            Norwalk, Connecticut 06852

**Please send me the following titles:**

| Quantity | Book Number | Price |
|----------|-------------|-------|
| ———— | ———— | ———— |
| ———— | ———— | ———— |
| ———— | ———— | ———— |
| ———— | ———— | ———— |
| ———— | ———— | ———— |

In the event we are out of stock on any of your selections, please list alternate titles below.

| | | |
|----------|-------------|-------|
| ———— | ———— | ———— |
| ———— | ———— | ———— |
| ———— | ———— | ———— |
| ———— | ———— | ———— |

Postage/Handling ————
I enclose..... ————

**FOR U.S. ORDERS,** add 50¢ for the first book and 10¢ for each additional book to cover cost of postage and handling. Buy five or more copies and we will pay for shipping. Sorry, no C.O.D.'s.

**FOR ORDERS SENT OUTSIDE THE U.S.A.**
Add $1.00 for the first book and 25¢ for each additional book. **PAY BY** foreign draft or money order drawn on a U.S. bank, payable in U.S. ($) dollars.
☐Please send me a free catalog.

NAME _____
                  (Please print)

ADDRESS _____

CITY _____ STATE_____ ZIP _____
Allow Four Weeks for Delivery